THE FIRE WITHIN

Jim Taylor
with Kristine Setting Clark

THE FIRE

Jim Taylor
with Kristine Setting Clark

TRIUMPH
B · O · O · K · S

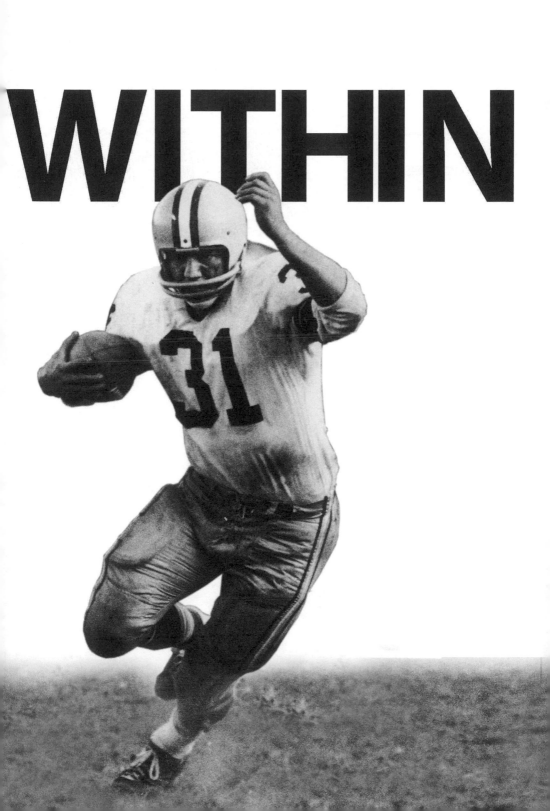

Triumph Books and colophon are registered trademarks of Random House, Inc.

Library of Congress Cataloging-in-Publication Data

Taylor, Jim, 1935–
  The fire within / Jim Taylor with Kristine Setting Clark.
    p. cm.
  Includes bibliographical references.
  ISBN-13: 978-1-60078-344-9
  ISBN-10: 1-60078-344-9
  1. Taylor, Jim, 1935– 2. Football players—United States—Biography. I. Clark, Kristine Setting, 1950– II. Title.
  GV939.T32A3 2010
  796.332092—dc22
  [B]

                                                          2010026139

This book is available in quantity at special discounts for your group or organization. For further information, contact:

Triumph Books
542 South Dearborn Street
Suite 750
Chicago, Illinois 60605
(312) 939-3330
Fax (312) 663-3557
www.triumphbooks.com

Printed in U.S.A.
ISBN: 978-1-60078-344-9
Design by Patricia Frey

Contents

Third Quarter: From Green Bay to New Orleans

Fourth Quarter: Life After Football

Appendix: Vignettes, Write-Ups, and Stats

Foreword

It has been said that Jim Taylor was one of the greatest fullbacks in football history. I am a testament to that statement. A sportswriter from the *Green Bay Gazette* once said of Jim Taylor: "Taylor came, he saw and he conquered."

Jim Taylor's legend remains as strong as the body-scattering runs that lifted him to prominence as one of the Green Bay Packers' most significant offensive weapons throughout the Lombardi era. Paired with former Notre Dame player and Heisman Trophy winner Paul Hornung, Vince Lombardi referred to them as "Thunder [Taylor] and Lightning [Hornung]."

Jim carried the ball with incredible power and force. He ran around, over, and through linemen and defensive backs alike. He was so intimidating that opponents were often afraid to tackle him. Taylor would carry the ball 25 to 30 times per game and totally wear out the defense.

Taylor rushed for more than 1,000 yards in five consecutive seasons (1960 to 1964) and helped the Packers win four NFL titles plus a game against the AFL champion Kansas City Chiefs that later became known as Super Bowl I. In 1962 he surpassed the great Jim Brown for the rushing title and was named league MVP.

The NFL of the 1950s and 1960s was a completely different entity than the polished, image-conscious icon that it has become today. Back then there were few rules and many cheap tactics. Punching, whip-kicking, head slapping, and more were commonplace in the game. Jim was not immune to them. As one of the most dangerous weapons on the Packers, he drew attention and cheap shots from the most vicious enforcers and still found his way to the end zone.

An All-American at LSU, Taylor discovered that it was the violence of football that appealed to him most. The idea of physically dominating other men and surviving explosive, violent battles on the gridiron against opponents fueled an amazing NFL career that led him to the Pro Football Hall of Fame.

Jim was definitely a man ahead of his time. He was one of the few men to utilize weight training and isometrics in his daily physical regimen, because LSU (one of the few colleges to do so at that time) had incorporated the use of weights into its athletic programs, though Jim was training with weights as early as junior high school. Back in those days, calisthenics and running were the only forms of exercise in professional football.

I personally was in awe of his superior athletic abilities and skill—especially when watching him on game films. He was basically unstoppable. The caliber of strength and explosiveness that he possessed was phenomenal.

In 1967 Jim retired from professional football. He had stood at the forefront of the Green Bay offense for nine years and helped the team become world champions.

In 1976 Jim was inducted into the Pro Football Hall of Fame. His presenter was Marie Lombardi, the wife of his former coach, Vince Lombardi.

No. 31 will forever be remembered as one of the elite who donned the Green Bay Packers uniform.

—Bart Starr

Introduction

His face isn't imprinted on money, and his head isn't immortalized on Mount Rushmore. He might be forgotten by everyone but history teachers and distant relatives. But James Polk is still one of my favorite presidents.

In only four years, Polk added the land that would become seven states—including the entire Pacific Coast. He believed in manifest destiny, that Americans had a divine mission to push West with a resolute tenacity.

By the time Jim Taylor suited up for the Packers, the West was won, but the battle for the other three points on the compass had just begun. Taylor was a north-south runner, a stomping fullback with straightaway power who hit the line with splintering force. Vince Lombardi called him the best back he ever saw at running to daylight, but it seemed he enjoyed running over linebackers just as much. He was a human freight train. A whistle heralded not his arrival but his departure, after the grass was strewn with defenders who had either bodies or spirits broken.

The 1960s were an era of thrilling running backs: Gale Sayers, Leroy Kelly, Jim Brown. While not a breakaway runner, Jim Taylor provided as much excitement as them all—but in shorter, more violent bursts.

He perceived every play as an examination of his manhood. He spat, elbowed, and battled his way to five consecutive 1,000-yard seasons.

Lombardi lauded him for his year-round dedication to conditioning and used him as a model for his championship Packers. Taylor also rarely fumbled, averaging only one fumble every 64 carries, better than Walter Payton (51), Jim Brown (47), and Eric Dickerson (34).

Taylor led the Packers to four NFL championships and one Super Bowl. The one place he didn't finish first was in career rushing yards. When he retired, Taylor ranked third behind Brown and Joe Perry. But there was significance in the chase. His quest for the rushing record revealed a fundamental truth about the sport. Jim Taylor is a reminder that football will always be a game for men who take pride in their own power and toughness.

—Steve Sabol, president of NFL Films

The Early Years

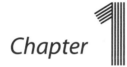

Nothing Was Easy

I was born in Baton Rouge, Louisiana, on September 20, 1935. My mother and father, Alice and Clark Taylor, were the best parents any child could ever hope to have. They had very little in the way of money and personal possessions, but they gave my brothers and me a great deal of love and affection. My father was originally from Ferriday, Louisiana, and my mother was from Woodville, Mississippi.

We lived in what was known back then as a shotgun home at 304 South 18th Street in the heart of Baton Rouge. I was the middle sibling of three boys. The first child, Clark, was two years my senior, and my other brother, Webb, was two years my junior.

My father was a tall, thin man who, at the young age of 15, became inflicted with rheumatoid arthritis. The crippling disease made it difficult for him to work; therefore, he was very limited in what he could do. He had worked as a watchman for many years, but when the Depression hit, he could not find a job.

My mother, on the other hand, had no more than a third-grade education and was forced to become the breadwinner of the family. Throughout the Depression we were given ration stamps. The stamps were used to purchase coffee, meat, and other groceries. At that time, a loaf of bakery-baked bread was a nickel.

My mom worked at a place called Kean's Dry Cleaners, located several blocks from our home. She worked as a seamstress in the uniforms department with six other women. Her weekly wages averaged between $25 and $30. At the end of the day, after all the workers had punched out for the evening, my mother would stay behind to clean and sweep before going home. She did this every night just to earn a few dollars more. Hard work had become a way of life for her.

When my brothers and I were very young, my father suffered from heart disease that eventually claimed his life. He passed away at the young age of 57. Unfortunately, that same gene that gave him heart disease was passed along to both my brothers and me.

My young mother was a widow left to raise three boys—ages 12, 10, and 8—on her own. As young as my siblings and I were, we never refused a job that would help support my mother and help to put food on the table. It was a difficult time for all of us, as nothing came easy.

Mama was now not only the breadwinner but also the disciplinarian. She was a small, stocky woman who taught me the value of obedience and self-control—qualities that I would respect for the rest of my life.

Once in a while my brothers and I would play at the railroad station. We could catch crawfish there. One time while fishing, we fell into some holes and were covered with oil and soot from head to toe. When we returned home, we hid behind the house because we knew what was coming. When Mama saw us, all she said was, "Go pick out your switches and bring them to me." And we did. When Mama said jump, we would ask how high.

Even though she had no education and was without money, she had high ambitions for her three sons. Her biggest dream was for all of us to earn college degrees. She felt that this would help us have a much easier and successful life than she had. Her dream came true.

Clark worked his way through LSU and LSU Law School and went on to become a successful lawyer and real-estate developer in Baton Rouge. My younger brother Webb also worked his way through LSU and earned a degree in accounting. He went on to a successful accounting career working for the Louisiana Department of Transportation. I was fortunate enough to be awarded an athletic scholarship to LSU and graduated with a bachelor's degree in Physical Education and Coaching. As a matter of fact, at the end of the 1958 Packers season, I reenrolled at LSU in January 1959 to complete my student teaching and receive my degree. To this day, I cherish that college degree more than any athletic award that I have received.

Mama not only wanted us to get good educations but also to possess and use good manners. Every Sunday we attended Sunday School and church. We all said, "Yes, ma'am" and "No, ma'am" and "Yes, sir" and "No, sir." Not only was this a reflection on Mama, but it also showed that we were accountable for who we were at a very young age.

Chapter

Helping Out Mama

During this time, a woman by the name of Mrs. Matheny gave my brother Clark and me newspaper routes. Clark was in junior high school, while Webb and I were attending Dufrocq Elementary School. Webb was still too young to work.

Neither Clark nor I were actually old enough to work directly with the *Morning Advocate*, the Baton Rouge daily paper, so we worked through Mrs. Matheny. We needed social security numbers to work, and we couldn't apply for them until we were 12 years old. Her husband at the time was still in the service, and she needed someone to deliver and collect for the papers. Our routes were in the evening, and we each made $4 to $5 a week, including 20 percent of our weekly collections.

Clark and I also picked up jobs mowing lawns, and when we would get the chance, we would sweep out one of the many laundry facilities in the area.

Never passing up an opportunity to make a few bucks, my brother and I also delivered phone books. We had a black four-door Model A Ford sedan that my mom would drive around as we dropped off the phone books.

Two years later—and old enough to *officially* have newspaper routes—we were hired by the *Morning Advocate* to deliver the daily news. I was in Baton Rouge Junior High School at the time. My mom would get us up at 4:00 or 5:00 AM, and we would fold our papers, stuff them into our newspaper sacks, and deliver them to approximately 200 homes *every day of the week.*

Having a newspaper route also required that we pay for each newspaper that we delivered. At the end of the month it was up to us to collect the money for the papers from the subscribers and pay back what we owed to the *Morning Advocate*, and whatever money was left over became our wages for the month. If we failed to collect from a subscriber, then it became our loss…not the company's. I made sure to always collect from everyone. It was like having my own little business.

Upon our return from slinging newspapers, my mother would always have a hot breakfast waiting for us. As soon as we walked through the door, we could smell the aroma of fresh homemade biscuits being baked in the oven. Mom would always serve them with sour cream and homemade jellies and preserves.

After breakfast, we walked to school. While attending Baton Rouge Junior High there were really not any organized sports to speak of. We played Ping-Pong or billiards, went bowling, or played sports at the YMCA. The cost per year to join the Y was only a couple of dollars. There was a track where we could run, basketball courts for games, and a place to interact with peers and friends.

When the school bell rang at 3:00, my brothers and I proceeded to our second and third jobs of the day. After school we mowed lawns, and in the evening we sold hot tamales from Muffaletta's Hot Tamale Kitchen on North Boulevard.

The workers from Muffaletta's would begin getting the tamales ready in the early morning. Their daily ritual would consist of cutting the shucks to prepare the tamales. Next they would soak and slow-cook them all day, and by the time we arrived, they were packed and ready to go.

We were each given a pushcart that was insulated with stainless steel. We picked up the tamales around 4:00 in the afternoon and sold them on the corner of Government and 19th Streets. Our customers were either coming home from work or going to a baseball game at City Park. We sold the tamales for about 35¢–40¢ a dozen and made a nickel for each dozen we sold.

The land around City Park Lake was a nine-hole golf course. We would caddy for 50¢ a round. During World War II, there were many Second Lieutenants who played golf, and if we were lucky, we would carry two bags for two of them. That would give us a whole dollar for the round!

Next door to Muffaletta's was Slim's Barber Shop, where we would get our hair cut for 25¢. Slim let us shine shoes at his shop, where we would make a nickel a shine.

Coke bottles would bring in 2¢, and milk bottles would bring in 5¢. My brothers and I would also stop at Benny's Bar for extra money. We would go around to the back of the bar, pick up the empty beer bottles, then go to the front of the bar and sell them back to Benny.

At the LSU football games, we would sell peanuts and Cokes to the fans. The Cokes were in bottles back then, so we would have to open them with an opener and pour the Coke into paper cups. Peanuts sold for 10¢ a bag, and we made 1¢ off of each bag sold. Including tips, we would sometimes make $10 or $11 a night. Back then, that was a great deal of money. The following day we would get up early in the morning and go back to the stadium to look under the bleachers to see if we could find any money that may have fallen out of the fans' pockets during the previous night's game.

When we brought home good money from LSU, we used to go to Astoria across from Dufrocq Elementary School. They made the best burgers in town. Mama gave each of us enough money for two hamburgers and a drink for a job well done.

On Saturdays mama would give my brothers and me 15¢ each to go to the Tivoli Theatre. It was 9¢ to get in. That would get us a cartoon, a newsreel, a serial, and a main feature. Popcorn was 5¢, and candy was a penny. It didn't get any better than that.

Before and after dinner was time set aside for homework. It was difficult for me to adjust the year my father died. My grades suffered, and I was forced to repeat the fourth grade. Thanks to the kindness of our teachers, my brothers and I were given extra support at that difficult period in our young lives.

Our clothes were hand-me-downs, and if it were not for the Goodfellows, Salvation Army, and some of the other charitable organizations, we would not have had a Christmas. These wonderful people brought my family sacks of rice and potatoes, a fruit basket, and a few toys. I will always be thankful to them for their charitable donations.

Our family had some good friends by the name of Seale. One year they bought their sons new suits for Easter and gave my brothers and me their old suits. Those were the first suits that we ever owned, and we were so glad to have received them.

Mrs. Cangelosi gave us the job of sweeping the floors of the Crescent Cleaners on the corner of Government and 18th Streets. We pocketed $3 a week.

If there was no work to be found, Mrs. Bombet and Mrs. Hart would find us work. They were both wonderful people. The Harts owned the movie theater and were prominent people in Baton Rouge.

My brothers and I would go over to their homes, and they would have us water the grass, clean up trash—basically whatever work they could find for us. We made 10¢ to 15¢.

We were always willing to do anything for anybody to earn a few bucks. We did not want handouts. We always wanted to earn our money with whatever work would come our way. Growing up, we were taught to do the right thing and that there was no free ride.

There were always ways for kids to make money in those days; they just had to be driven to do so. I guess my fire within began at a very young age and became part of my internal makeup.

Chapter

My Love of Sports

From an early age I loved sports. My first love was not football but actually basketball. Having no father with whom to throw a football or baseball, I shot basketball alone. I used to sneak out of my house at night and shoot baskets in the moonlight.

I began to experiment with strength conditioning in junior high. Lifting weights was not popular at that time, but it turned out to be my greatest asset and carried me all the way through to the pros.

In my freshman year at Baton Rouge High School in 1951, I made the varsity basketball team and received my first varsity letter. In my senior year, our team won the state championship. I have many wonderful memories of my teammates, our hours of practice, and the many hard-fought games we played.

During my junior year in 1953, I made All-City, All-District, and All-State in basketball as a point guard. Even with all the accolades, I was very shy. My focus was on basketball and pool. Pool was a way for me to relax and to be with my friends. I played pickup games at the YMCA. I also continued with my strength training.

One of my high school coaches noticed my burning desire to compete in athletics and asked me to try out for the football team. I was only in 10th grade at the time. I did make the squad but saw very little action. It wasn't until my senior year that I began to blossom.

I developed my basketball skills at the YWCA, and in the summer I played American Legion baseball. Sports became a year-round obsession for me.

Baton Rouge High School and Istrouma High School were the two big rivals in Baton Rouge in the 1950s. While I was playing football my senior year, there was a sophomore star at Istrouma High by the name of Billy Cannon. We competed against each other throughout our high school years together but we were teammates at LSU. Billy won the Heisman Trophy in 1959—the year after I graduated from college. He went on to play for the Houston Oilers and the Oakland Raiders. After his playing days were over, Billy became a dentist. Throughout the years, we have remained good friends.

At the close of my senior year at BRHS in 1954, I was named First Team All-District, All-State, and First Team All-American in both basketball and football. I played in the All-American basketball game in Murray, Kentucky, and in the North-South Senior Bowl in Mobile, Alabama. I received MVP honors in the Senior Bowl that year. The idea of a team concept really began to solidify and come together for me.

I always felt that I was a much better high school basketball player than a football player. In my later years I would be inducted into the National High School Hall of Fame for my high school basketball career. When it was time to go to college, I received far more scholarship offers for basketball than I did for football. The reason I chose to play football was because LSU offered me a football scholarship. That meant that I could go to college and still be close enough to help my mother. Big things would happen for me at LSU.

Chapter

LSU

I entered LSU in the fall of 1954. I made the freshman team, and athletically I felt pretty confident about my skills and ability to play. In the 1950s freshmen were not allowed to play on the varsity squad.

Back in those days the freshman team only played three games per season. That year we played Ole Miss, Tulane, and Mississippi State.

By the time December had rolled around, my grades had fallen by the wayside. I was forced to take a leave from LSU and attend Hinds Junior College during my sophomore year in order to raise my grades. I played football for Hinds in 1955. Our season consisted of only nine games.

I buckled down and returned to LSU to play football in my junior and senior years. Coach Paul Dietzel was the new head football coach at LSU, and coach Charlie McClendon was my defensive coach. We played both offense and defense back then. I was the team's middle linebacker and running back. I was also the defensive captain.

One summer I took a summer job with the Noble Drilling Company in Cut Off, Louisiana. It was and still is a family owned and operated company now based in New Orleans. I signed on to be an oil-field deckhand—aka roughneck. The reason I took this job was because I wanted to make the most money that I could in the shortest period of time.

The job consisted of 12 hours a day on a drilling rig in the marsh. I wore an aluminum hard hat and steel-toed shoes. The crew was made up of a driller, two roughnecks, a derrick man, and a tool pusher. I did not possess any experience. I got myself an apartment near the job site. In those days we took our lunches out in brown bags and never had time to eat them. We usually ate our lunches on the way *back* to the dock.

It was an extremely dangerous job. It would take hours just to change a drill bit. I worked seven days a week, and I was the youngest worker there. The rest of the crew was made up of grown men, and this was their regular year-round job.

I learned to grow up quickly in that job, and after working only one summer, I knew that it was something that I did not want to do for the rest of my life. I returned to LSU and trained even harder than before.

As a junior in 1956 at LSU, I played football, but sparingly. At that time I was not considered a playmaker. At 21, I hadn't yet reached my maximum size and weight. I was still developing, growing, and maturing.

In 1957 I was a senior, and my athletic endeavors on the football field began to be noticed. In the game against Georgia Tech, I scored all of LSU's points. We beat them by a score of 20–13. We finished the 1957 season with a 5–5 record.

That same year I was an All-American and MVP of the Blue-Gray football game. I was also the top SEC scorer with 86 points, I had set a new two-year scoring record at LSU with 145 points, and I was the first to repeat as SEC scoring leader in 25 years. I was also the eighth leading rusher in the nation. The write-up I was given in my LSU college yearbook stated: "Top individual honor went to 200-pound fullback Jimmy Taylor, who scored more points than any LSU footballer since the fabulous Steve Van Buren and who led the SEC as scoring champion."

I felt it to be quite an honor to be compared to LSU's Van Buren.

To be noticed by the pros, you really have to step it up a notch. Apparently I did just that. I was the second pick of the Green Bay Packers in the 1958 NFL Draft. I have to admit that this was probably at least partly because our assistant coach at LSU, Abner Wimberly—who had played with the Packers—had put in a good word about me to Jack Vainisi without my knowledge. Vainisi was the head scout for Green Bay and a genius at drafting players.

Jack contacted me and sent me an application to play pro football. That's what they did in those days. I sent back the application with the following letter attached:

November 19, 1957

Dear Mr. Vainisi

Reference to your letter dated November 11, 1957. I am very much interested in playing professional football. Football is a great sport, and I enjoy playing it. Yes, I would be interested in playing with the Green Bay Packers. My military status is 1A, Category 4. Yes, I will be able to play pro ball before entering the service. I prefer either the United States or Canada. Fullback is a position I feel I can play better.

Sincerely,

Jim Taylor

Baton Rouge, Louisiana

When Vainisi called to tell me that the Packers had drafted me, I told him that I didn't even know where Green Bay was, much less the fact that they had a team!

The All-Star Game that year was played at Northwestern. Vainisi picked me up and drove me there three weeks prior in order to practice for the game.

On August 15, 1958, the College All-Stars played the league champion Detroit Lions. The All-Stars won by a score of 35–19. After the game, Jack picked me up and drove me to Green Bay for the start of my professional career.

The Green Bay Packers

Chapter

Coach Ray "Scooter" McLean

At the end of the 1957 season, the Packers had won only three games and lost nine. Green Bay fans frantically shouted for coach Lisle Blackbourn's resignation. The pressure became too much for Blackbourn. He soon quit the team and returned to Marquette University to coach football.

Before he departed, he asked Bart Starr to leave with him and become his quarterbacks coach at Marquette. He told Bart that he (Starr) was going to have a "tough time" making it as a pro quarterback. That shows how much Blackbourn knew. Luckily, Starr didn't listen to him.

In 1958 assistant coach Ray "Scooter" McLean succeeded Blackbourn as the new Packers coach. Ray had become an assistant coach with Green Bay during the 1951 3–9 season under the leadership of coach Gene Ronzani.

The year 1958 was also the year *I* began my career with the Packers—and I arrived with some damn good credentials. I'd been All-America at LSU and Most Valuable Player in the Senior Bowl. Even though Green Bay drafted me in the second round, I sat on the bench for the first 10 games of a 12-game schedule. Scooter McLean had been an old Chicago Bears running back and was with the AAFC Chicago Rockets when the Packers hired him. Green Bay was grasping at straws after many losing seasons, and McLean had a reputation as a good assistant coach, but as a head coach he was in over his head.

In today's NFL, fullbacks are guys who do little more than block for the tailback and pick up blitzing linemen. But in the 1950s and 1960s, all the great backs were fullbacks, and they did everything from blocking to catching passes to running the ball.

When I joined the Packers, former Notre Dame player and Heisman Trophy winner Paul Hornung was their halfback.

It was thought that Paul would become their biggest star. At Notre Dame he had become a triple threat on offense. He could run, throw, and catch the ball, not to mention the fact that he was also a great field-goal kicker. He had been such a great quarterback for the Fighting Irish that the Packers traded Tobin Rote, their longtime starting quarterback who passed for more than 11,000 yards, and signed Hornung. Upon signing his three-year contract, Paul received an annual salary of $17,500 plus a signing bonus of $2,500. That was more than many of the vets on the team were getting paid.

The only problem was that once Paul suited up for game day, it was obvious that he didn't have a strong enough passing arm to be a pro quarterback. On top of that, he didn't possess the speed to become a great running back or receiver. For a while it looked as though there was no place for him on the team. So there were no guarantees, especially for a second-round draft choice like myself!

Back then there were no high-profile or high-priced agents who negotiated for the players. Players were responsible for their own negotiations with the team, and the process was not always easy.

At the beginning of the '58 Packers season an air of optimism seemed to blanket the team. Prior to our first game, Coach McLean told the *Green Bay Press-Gazette*, "We're not shooting for just a good season; we're going after the championship."

That line of thinking quickly changed to resentment and despair as we lost the first game, tied the second, and then continued to lose nine of our last 10 games. Our 1–10–1 record was the worst in the history of the franchise.

Sportswriter Art Daly of the *Green Bay Press-Gazette* defined the Packers' season in one sentence: "The Packers had overwhelmed one opponent, underwhelmed ten and whelmed one."

After losing to Chicago, Baltimore, and Washington and tying Detroit, we once again were up against the undefeated Baltimore Colts, and to make matters even worse, this time the game was played at Memorial Stadium in Baltimore.

The date was November 2, 1958, and it was a game we would never forget. Anything that could go wrong went wrong—both offensively and defensively. On top of it all, it was cold and raining. As the stadium lights pierced through the chilly, damp stadium, an eerie darkness prevailed over the misty field.

The Baltimore crowd was relentless, to say the least. One sportswriter made the comment that "Municipal Stadium is the world's largest outdoor insane asylum."

The Colts offense was just as intimidating and known for tearing opposing defenses to shreds. With a backfield that included the brilliance of quarterback Johnny Unitas, Lenny Moore, Raymond Berry, and Alan Ameche, and a defensive line that was held by All-Pros Gino Marchetti at end and Art Donovan at tackle, they were practically impossible to beat.

As the Packers' offensive backfield jogged onto the field, it would be Babe Parilli, Jim Ringo, and Billy Howton who would start for Green Bay, while the second team—Bart Starr, Hornung, and I—watched from the sideline.

We fumbled the ball on the opening kickoff, and the Colts went ahead 7–0. After fumbling the second kickoff, the Colts led 14–0. We got the ball back for a short time and again fumbled, allowing Baltimore to score for an unprecedented third time. By early in the second quarter, Green Bay was losing 21–0. When the second half began, we were trailing by four touchdowns.

But just prior to the end of the half, Unitas drove the Colts downfield toward another touchdown. He first passed to Moore and then to Berry two plays in succession. Baltimore was on our 19-yard line, and our Green Bay defense had no way of stopping them.

On the next play, Unitas dropped back, his receivers all covered. He had no alternative but to run up the middle. One of our cornerbacks, John Symank, smacked Unitas to the ground and then kneed him in the ribs. The Colts' backup quarterback, George Shaw, took over for Unitas and threw a TD pass, making the score 28–0 at the half.

In the meantime, the Colts were infuriated by Unitas' injuries and vowed to take revenge on Symank and the rest of the Packers squad. They scored three times after the second-half kickoff.

By that time, a few of the players had decided that the game was all but over and that they would coast through the final 20 minutes of the competition. As long as the "coasting" wasn't obvious, Coach McLean didn't mind. A few of the guys even went so far as to contemplate taking a sideline policeman's gun and shooting the Colts' mascot, Dixie, a beautiful white horse that galloped across the field every time Baltimore scored. The final score of the game was Colts 56, Packers 0. It was the worst defeat in the history of the Packers franchise.

Green Bay Press-Gazette sports editor Art Daley had spent the day watching his Packers from the press box. To say that he was furious would be an understatement. The following day, his outrage was clear in his column, which read, "The second half of the game was an almost complete lack of effort and their performance was the biggest quit in Packer history."

The following week we played the Bears in Chicago. Once again we came up on the losing end of the stick—Bears 24, Green Bay 10. The only bright spot in the game was when McLean called on me to get into the huddle. I scored our only touchdown—our first in eight quarters.

We continued our downfall by losing 20–7 at home to the Rams, 33–12 to the 49ers, and 24–14 to the Lions in Detroit on Thanksgiving Day.

After sitting out the first 10 games of the season, I finally got my chance to start and play in the final two. I took over from Hornung as starting fullback for both games. Up until then I'd only played on kickoff returns and gone down on kickoffs and punts, all on special teams.

On December 7, 1958, we played against the 49ers in San Francisco. I gained more than 100 yards in that game, but we still lost by a score of 48–21.

We played our final regular-season game against the Rams in Los Angeles. Once again I gained more than 106 yards on 22 carries, but we still lost. Final score: Rams 34, Packers 20.

I ended up with only 247 rushing yards for the season—almost all of them in those last two games. I just hadn't been given the opportunity until then. But after that, I felt I could make it as a running back in the National Football League—despite our 1–10–1 record for the season.

The Packers sat at the bottom of the NFL and hadn't produced a winning season since 1947. Long gone were the glory years of the Packers from 1929 to 1931, and long gone were the heroes from the past—Curly Lambeau, Johnny "Blood" McNally, Clark Hinkle, Cal Hubbard, and Don Hutson, to name a few.

Our humiliating 56–0 loss to Baltimore was the straw that broke the camel's back. The abuse that was unleashed from the fans and the media continued throughout the rest of the 1958 season. With ineffective quarterbacking, an ineffective defense, and an ineffective coaching staff, the media had a field day criticizing the organization. It seemed that everyone loved McLean as a person, but as a coach the team failed to respond to his direction.

Poor physical-conditioning training and lackluster practices were the norm. One day while at practice, McLean called for wind sprints. After running a few laps, our veteran receiver Billy Howton yelled out to Scooter, "Come on, Scooter, we need to save our legs for Sunday!"

With that, Scooter smiled, blew his whistle, and ended practice.

Instead of utilizing film reviews as a teaching tool, the coaching staff basically just ran the film. The film sessions were useless. Scooter may not have known a lot of things, but he *did* know offensive football.

He adopted an offensive system, which dated back to the 1930s when University of Chicago coach Clark Shaughnessy revamped the T formation to improve the passing game. George Halas later incorporated the offensive and ended up winning four NFL titles in the 1940s, when McLean was playing for the Bears. As the Packers' coach, Scooter utilized the same offensive system but added his own wrinkles…a great deal of them. The one-time one-inch-thick playbook had developed into a four-inch-thick playbook made up of intricate diagrams and plays that were so complicated that I couldn't figure them out. The system required the offense to learn different blocking assignments on *every play*. To further complicate matters, the staff would change the assignments from week to week, therefore allowing for many missed blocks.

Apparently, McLean's system was just as bad as Blackbourn's had been. It definitely was confusing to me. Even though I had gained more than 100 yards in each of the final two games of the season, I still wasn't sure what I was supposed to be doing out there!

I was told that McLean was a much better guy than Blackbourn but just as bad a coach. During the preseason, McLean announced that we would all be on the honor system as far as bed check went. For Max McGee and Paul Hornung, that statement was considered a license to party.

The word *curfew* meant only two things to Max and Paul—either total exhaustion or 4:00 AM, whichever came first.

McLean lacked the capacity to discipline. There were few rules, and curfews were flexible and routinely ignored. He became the players' friend—one of the guys—instead of the coach and leader. He would even play poker with us on the eve before a game. He allowed the players to establish and supervise training rules. He also appointed a committee of players to advise him of team problems, not realizing that some of those appointed *were the problems!*

There was no dress code. We wore whatever we wanted on the road. Scooter himself was rarely seen in a coat and tie.

Jerry Kramer once said, "I think every man on the club took advantage of him. There was no dress code, and when some players wore T-shirts to away games, they looked as sloppy as they played."

Many times players skipped team meetings—often unnoticed by Coach, who had a bad habit of daydreaming when the film projector was running. It's even been said that he once fell asleep in the middle of a film session and awoke to find himself the only one left in the room.

Bart Starr, who was accustomed to discipline, was very uncomfortable with Scooter. He saw no rational pattern to his play selection or use of players.

Starr said, "If you made an error you went out, and if the other guy made an error you went back in. Not only does it test your resolve, it tests your reasoning, where you're going wrong. You're not accomplishing what you want to."

Hornung was so distraught with the coach and team that he wanted to be traded and even thought about quitting pro football.

Paul stated, "It was very individual. Those guys in Green Bay that year didn't give a shit about winning or losing."

What was ironic about our 1–10–1 record was the fact that the majority of the pieces of a winning team had already been in place—just not the *right* pieces in the *right* places. Bart, Paul, and I had spent the majority of the 1958 NFL season on the bench.

McLean was a friend to many of the local sportswriters, and they were easy on him when it came to writing about the Packers in Monday's early edition. Unlike many other coaches, he never refused an interview from the press or ever raised his voice at them in anger. When we got beat by Baltimore 56–0, Scooter's response was, "Well, you know, what the hell."

That's the kind of guy he was.

Scooter McLean resigned from the Packers organization following the worst season in Green Bay history and before the Green Bay board of directors could fire him. He went on to become an assistant coach in Detroit. That was the good news.

The bad news was that the January NFL meetings were just around the corner, and the Packers still hadn't named a head coach.

With time running out, Green Bay administrator Jack Vainisi contacted the offensive coach of the New York Giants and told him to apply for the head coaching position with Green Bay. Vainisi then suggested to the Packers' executive committee that they should first consult commissioner Bert Bell and Cleveland Browns head coach Paul Brown in regard to their choice for the job. The committee took Vainisi's advice and contacted both Bell and Brown, who unanimously chose the relatively unknown offensive coach with the Giants—a man by the name of Vincent Thomas Lombardi. Taking that chance turned out to be the best decision ever made in the history of the Packers franchise.

On January 28, 1959, when team president Dominic Olejniczak recommended to the committee that Lombardi be named the new coach for the Green Bay Packers, a longtime committee member by the name of John Torinus replied, "Who the hell is Vince Lombardi?"

The committee and the rest of the world quickly found out who and what Vince Lombardi was. Only hours after his arrival in Green Bay on

February 2, 1959, Lombardi told the committee, "I want it understood that I am in complete command here!"

Two days later, the Packers officially gave Lombardi the title of both coach and general manager of the Green Bay Packers. A dynasty was about to begin.

Chapter

The Italian from Brooklyn

Vincent Thomas Lombardi was born on June 11, 1913, in Brooklyn, NY. He was the first of Henry and Matilda Lombardi's five children. Henry was an Italian butcher, and like all good Italians Vince was raised a devout Catholic. He even studied the priesthood for two years before transferring to St. Francis Preparatory High School, where he became a star fullback on their football team.

In 1933 Vince was accepted at New York City's Fordham University. After a year on the freshman team, varsity football coach "Sleepy" Jim Crowley (a Knute Rockne protégé and one of the famed Four Horsemen) made the 170-pound Vince a guard on Fordham's offensive line, which was named the Seven Blocks of Granite. Off the field he was just as successful. In 1937 he graduated cum laude with a major in business.

For the next two years, Vince worked at a finance company, enrolled in evening classes at Fordham's law school, and played semipro football with Delaware's Wilmington Clippers. In 1939 he took a teaching position and coaching job at St. Cecilia High School in Englewood, NJ. Vince taught

Latin, algebra, physics, and chemistry and coached the football, basketball, and baseball teams. He did all that for a whopping $1,700 per year.

In 1940 Lombardi married Marie Planitz. They had a son, who they named Vince (not junior) and a daughter, Susan.

The older Vince left St. Cecilia in 1947 to coach at Fordham University. In his first year, he coached Fordham's freshman football team and was an assistant coach for the varsity team the next year.

In 1949 Earl "Colonel Red" Blaik (then football coach for the United States Military Academy at West Point and considered the best coach in the country at the time) hired Vince to manage the team's varsity defensive line. Working 17-hour days with Blaik helped refine Vince's leadership skills. Blaik taught Lombardi to stick with clear-cut plays (simple blocking and tackling), to strive for perfect execution, and to conduct himself respectfully on the field.

In 1954 Vince left West Point to take an assistant coaching position with the New York Giants. Their head coach was a former classmate of Lombardi's by the name of Jim Lee Howell. Vince was in charge of the Giants' defensive strategy. The previous season, the Giants' record was a dismal 3–9, not to mention they had the lowest number of points in the league. Only three years after Vince's arrival the Giants were a championship team. His leadership directed the talents of football great Frank Gifford, who he switched from defense to offense. For each of the five years that Lombardi coached the Giants, Gifford was nominated as a halfback on the All-Pro team, and the Giants never experienced a losing season.

By 1958 the 45-year-old Lombardi was looking to become a head coach. He accepted a challenging five-year contract in Wisconsin as the general manager and head coach of a losing Green Bay Packers team. At the time, the Packers had no respect in professional football, for they had won only one game the previous year. Vince saw the team as a chance to prove both himself and his coaching abilities to professional football.

Lombardi held intense training camps to gear up for the 1959 season. He told his team, "Dancing is a contact sport. Football is a hitting sport."

He expected obedience, dedication, and 110 percent effort from each man, but he also made a promise to them—if they obeyed his rules and used his methods, they would be a championship team.

Three years later, Lombardi's promise came to be. On December 31, 1961, at Lambeau Field in Green Bay, Vince watched proudly as his Packers defeated the New York Giants 37–0 for the National Football League championship.

Despite long hours and fierce competition, Lombardi never put forth anything but his best effort. Just as he conditioned his men to be the best players in professional football, he challenged himself. Vince was constantly looking to implement new plays and game strategies. He even went so far as to change his players' jersey numbers before a game to confuse George "Papa Bear" Halas and his Chicago Bears. The Packers offensive line became so powerful that their running game was dubbed "the Green Bay Sweep."

In 1967, after nine phenomenal winning seasons with the Packers, Vince decided to retire as head coach, though he would still act as general manager. The Packers had dominated professional football under his direction, acquiring six division titles, five NFL championships, two Super Bowls, and a record of 98–30–4. Green Bay had become the standard by which all other teams were measured.

Chapter

Controlled Violence— That's Football!

Lombardi was in charge of trades and contractual negotiations for the Packers. He also made the decision as to who would get bonuses and for how much. Throughout his reign in Green Bay, the board of directors never once overturned any of his decisions.

Known as "the Innovator," Lombardi even gave the order that the Packers' uniforms were to be revamped. With the exception of the addition of the G helmet logo, which was added in 1961, the uniforms have never changed since. The logo was designed by equipment manager Dad Braisher at Lombardi's request.

Lombardi had a saying: "Winning isn't everything—it's the only thing!" When questioned about his philosophy on race relations, he said, "The only color on my team is Green Bay Packers."

Prior to the onset of the 1959 season, most of the sportswriters and other football "experts" predicted the once-proud Packers would again find themselves in the cellar of the Western Conference. Lombardi, although noted as a good coach, was expected to write off the '59 season as a "rebuild-ing year." But as a team, we had a far different outlook on the situation.

Just prior to the opening of training camp, Vince utilized his powers of persuasion to induce the players to accept his team philosophy. I can remember All-Pro center Jim Ringo requesting to be traded because he didn't want to play another year on a losing team. Lombardi's deter-mination, passion, and drive to win changed Jim's outlook on the new season.

When defensive end Bill Quinlan received the news that he had been traded from Cleveland to Green Bay, he threatened to quit. But after Lombardi once again incorporated his powers of persuasion by shrewdly complimenting Quinlan on what a fine player he was, Bill was ready to sign his contract.

It didn't take long to convince me that Lombardi knew what he was doing. He sent assistant coach Red Cochran to spend a month with me in Baton Rouge so I would know the offense by the time I got to training camp. But the reality of it all was that Lombardi was very, very tough to deal with. I signed my first contract for $9,500 with a $1,000 bonus—and believe me, I had to *earn* every penny of it! Back then there were 34 guys on the team, and I hung on and was determined to make it…and I did.

But it was Bart Starr who was totally convinced that Lombardi was the right person for the job. Starr said, "After hearing his philosophy on foot-ball, I asked myself, *Where have you been all my life?* His whole approach, the forcefulness of his voice, his carriage, and his very presence oozed confidence."

Paul Hornung was the player that Vince had to convince. Lombardi told the press, "Let's face it…Hornung is the guy who can make this Packer team go. He is a key player. In New York we built our offense around Frank Gifford. Here in Green Bay, we'll build it around Hornung."

Paul began his third season under his third head coach and had played three positions. Soon after Lombardi arrived, he met with Paul. Coach didn't pull any punches. He said, "I know your reputation here. I've inves-tigated you very carefully. You have done things here that you shouldn't have done, but I don't think you have done as many things as people say you have done."

Paul responded, "If that's the way they want to think, that's the way they will think."

Vince smiled and said, "I trust you, but just don't let me down. If you do, it will be your ass!"

After watching game films, Vince was convinced that Paul would become his new halfback—his Frank Gifford.

On the eve of July 23, 1959, prior to our first practice, Coach Lombardi explained to us his approach to winning. In that deep, gruff voice of his, he spoke directly and articulately to us: "Gentlemen, I have never been associated with a losing team, and I don't intend to start now. We are going to win some games. Do you know why? Because you are going to have confidence in me and my system. By being alert you are going to make fewer mistakes than your opponents. By working harder you are going to outexecute, outblock, and out-tackle every team that comes your way."

At that point, each and every player had taken notice of what was being said.

Lombardi continued, "I've never been a losing coach, and I don't intend to start here. There is nobody big enough to think that he has got the team made or can do what he wants. Trains and planes are going in and coming out of Green Bay every day, and he'll be on one of them. I won't. I'm going to find 36 men who have the pride to make any sacrifice to win. There are such men. If they're not here, I'll get them. If you are not one, if you don't want to play, then you might as well leave right now. I've been up here all year and have learned a lot. I know how the townspeople are and what they think of you men. And I know that in a small town you need definite rules and regulations, and anybody who breaks these will be taken care of in my own way. You may not be a tackle, you may not be a guard, you may not be a back, but you *will* be a professional!"

You could hear a pin drop. The players were in awe, and in the end, not a player walked out on the team.

Later on we found out that Lombardi had confided to split end Max McGee that he had been nervous as hell prior to delivering that speech. He really thought that when he returned to camp the next day that many of his players would be missing.

During this time our linebacker Ray Nitschke was serving his time in the army while training camp was in full swing. Prior to his armed forces duties, Ray had only one year under his belt with the Packers. He didn't catch up to the team until our first exhibition game against Washington in Greensboro, North Carolina. Ray's reputation for being belligerent and rebellious preceded him. When he arrived, Green Bay's equipment manager Dad Braisher pulled him aside and said, "Watch yourself, Ray. Don't do anything you shouldn't be doing. This guy Lombardi is really tough!"

After spending the last six months in the army, Ray wondered how much tougher Lombardi's workouts could be than what he had just been through. The answers came quickly as he observed players vomiting on the practice field and the massive weight loss among his teammates. On the first day of practice alone, Lombardi told linebacker Tom Bettis and defensive tackle Dave Hanner to lose 20 pounds in two weeks or "get the hell out of camp."

Ray took Lombardi's words lightly and, because of it, ended up playing behind Bettis for the entire year. Nitschke was confined to playing on the special teams unit. While sitting on the sideline, sometimes Ray used his benching as a learning experience. He watched Bettis as well as opposing linebackers, such as Chicago's Bill George and Detroit's Joe Schmidt, to see how they played their positions. But many times he just sat there and sulked.

At the end of the 1959 season, Lombardi and Nitschke were at odds. Vince explained to us his list of rules and the fines for each offense. At the top of the list were the bars that were now off limits to the team—especially the Piccadilly—along with "No standing at any bar."

"One thing that I will not stand for," said Vince, "is a player standing at a public bar. I don't care if he's drinking ginger ale and talking to a friend, it just doesn't look good if a fan sees him doing that. Instead, players must drink at a table or a booth."

Coach was also adamant when it came to being on time. Whether it was for meals, meetings, or workouts, every player quickly learned that "on time" meant 15 minutes earlier than scheduled. This became known as "Lombardi time."

"I believe that a man should be on time," said Coach. "Not a minute late, not 10 seconds late. I believe that a man who is late for meetings or for the bus won't run his pass routes right. He'll be sloppy."

Some of his other rules were just as strict and just as precise. He felt that players should stay off the rubbing table and out of the tub. He believed that they should play with a little pain. If a player was overweight, he had better lose it—and now.

To look like professionals, the players had to dress like professionals. Lombardi bought each and every player a green sport coat with a gold-encrusted Packers emblem on the breast pocket. The guys were instructed to wear their sport coat with a dress shirt and tie on the road, in hotels, and at meals. Improving public appearance was important to Coach.

Lombardi had one set of strict rules that applied to all the players. But when it came to motivating players, each player was different; therefore, he treated each player according to what motivated him individually. But when it came to demanding 100 percent out of each player and following his rules to the letter, everyone was treated the same—that meant no special players, no prima donnas, and no special treatment!

We soon found out that anyone breaking curfew would pay for it dearly. Lombardi's rule stated that curfew would be strictly enforced by 11:00 PM, and he wasn't kidding.

The first player to break curfew was Emlen Tunnell. He arrived back at the dorm at 11:05 PM one night. Vince immediately fined him $50 and, like wildfire, word got out to the rest of the team. But it seemed to take a little longer for it to sink into my head.

One night Vince came into my room. I was sitting on the edge of my bed with my socks and shorts on. The time was 11:00 PM.

"Jimmy, what time do you have?" asked Vince.

"I've got 11:00, sir," I answered.

"Jimmy, you're supposed to be in bed at 11:00, aren't you?"

"Yes, sir," I replied.

"Jimmy, that is going to cost you $25!"

I never made that mistake again!

Our practices were shorter than those of the Blackbourn and McLean eras—about 75 minutes—but the difference between theirs and Lombardi's was the intensity of the performance. It was far more demanding, and little time, if any, was lost and no effort was wasted.

On the first day of practice, Vince had the guys run laps. Noticing that two of his players were running lackadaisically and lethargically, Lombardi growled, "If you fellows don't want to give me 100 percent, get on up to the clubhouse and turn in your equipment!" The team quickly got the message. It was easier to put out 100 percent during practice than to have to deal with the consequences of not.

Another issue that Coach would not tolerate was a dropped ball on an easy pass. Any time a receiver dropped an easy pass, he would have to take a lap. Dropped passes soon became few and far between.

Lombardi called football "controlled violence," and he did not consider the phrase a contradiction of words. The violence was as important to him as the control. He distinguished controlled violence from brutality, which he said ultimately defeats itself, but he did not try to minimize the role of violence. To approach football any other way, he said, "would be idiotic."

He truly believed that pain was a means to an end. The art was in what pain created—tireless, fearless, unbeatable men. That became the standard for the Green Bay Packers.

One sportswriter said this about Vince: "Compared to Lombardi, Simon Legree was a gentle humanitarian."

Coach drove us relentlessly. There was the constant reiteration of how hard work would bring success. The combination of wind sprints on the grass and nutcracker drills were the toughest and most exhausting. Lombardi would shout at us during the sprints. He once told reporters, "Run! Run! Run! We may not have the best team in the league, but we'll sure have the best legs!"

It was no surprise when some of the guys began to drop weight. Tom Bettis went from 245 to 220, Bill Forester from 240 to 230, and Dave Hanner from 270 to 250. Hanner actually had to be hospitalized for sunstroke. Offensive end Gary Knafelc complained to Marie, Vince's wife, about the torture and abuse. Offering little sympathy for Knafelc, Marie responded with, "How would you like to live with him?"

Right from the beginning, Lombardi made personnel changes that put Hornung and me in the backfield with Boyd Dowler. He also gave us a simplified system that suited each of our talents. His philosophy was to keep it simple and to avoid mistakes. Lombardi didn't care whether the other team knew a certain play was coming or not. He realized that if we executed properly, we couldn't be stopped.

We had approximately 18 offensive plays, which equated to 10 runs and 8 passes—all called by Starr. The best one was called the Green Bay Sweep. Either Paul or I would get a handoff from Bart and take off around end, allowing guards Jerry Kramer and Fuzzy Thurston time to pull and get ahead of us.

Most of our success was when we ran it to the strong side—the side where tight end Ron Kramer could take on the linebackers. Either Paul or me would block the defensive end. We would find a hole and run to daylight.

When it came to studying Packers films, Vince was a fanatic. After deciding that Paul was going to be our left halfback, he was on the hunt for quarterback assistance. Starr had yet to develop, and Lombardi knew that the team needed more quarterback help. He acquired Lamar McHan from the Chicago Cardinals and made him his No. 1 quarterback with Joe Francis as his backup. Starr was relegated to third string. Changes were just beginning.

Chapter

The Packers Sweep— Lombardi's Signature Play

The Packers Sweep had become Lombardi's signature play—the one that we had practiced more than any other, refining it again and again until we all knew that we could run it any time against any opponent. Utilizing this play, guards Jerry Kramer and Fuzzy Thurston led the way for Hornung and me many times.

Like many of Lombardi's plays, the sweep relied on a minimum of deception but a maximum of effort. This is how it worked.

The pulling guards formed a convoy around end, with the lead guard taking out the cornerback and the offside guard picking up the middle linebacker or outside linebacker. The center executed a cutoff block on the defensive tackle, and the onside offensive tackle popped the defensive end and then sealed off the middle linebacker. The blocking back led the ball carrier into the hole with a down block on the defensive end, and the tight end drove the outside linebacker in the direction he wanted to go. If the linebacker made an inside move, the tight end rode him in that direction and the runner hit outside. If the linebacker went outside, the tight end moved with him, and the runner cut inside.

Because of the option blocking of the tight end and the runner's ability to cut inside or outside, the sweep was really two plays in one. Three, if you add the extra dimension of the halfback option pass off the sweep action.

What it was most however, was a four-yards-and-a-cloud-of-dust play perfectly suited to Green Bay's ball-control offense.

Hornung and I were big, mobile backs who were perfectly suited to run Lombardi's sweep. Though neither of us were particularly fast, both of us excelled at running under control—that is, reading the blocks of the pulling guards in front of us and then hitting the right hole.

The play made everybody work as a team, and it gave everyone enough responsibility that we all took it upon ourselves to do the best we could. It became the best play in football.

In our Packers playbook, the sweep was known as *49* when run to the right and *28* when run to the left. To opponents however, it didn't much matter to which side the play went. When Starr bent low in our Green Bay huddle and called out, "Fire, Brown Right, 49 Sweep, zone blocking, on two," we broke from the huddle exuding confidence.

Green Bay guards Jerry Kramer and Fuzzy Thurston loved the sweep because, among other things, it featured line play and brought offensive guards out of the obscurity they toiled in. Jerry said, "With his [Lombardi's] system, he made me proud to be an offensive lineman. Generally speaking, there's nothing more anonymous than playing guard. Once you have been announced in the lineups, you never again hear your name over the loud-speaker. But with Lombardi's offensive system, with the guards pulling and leading the attack, Fuzzy Thurston and I emerged from obscurity. Every time there'd be a photograph in the papers of Hornung or Taylor scoring a touchdown, which was pretty often, there'd either be me or Fuzzy or both of us in the picture, leading the way."

While the success of the sweep relied on each member of the offense, the pulling action of the guards was most essential. The guard who had the most difficult assignment was the off guard, the guard who had to pull farthest away from the play while still getting to the outside in time to lead the convoy.

The cutoff block made by our center Jim Ringo was just as difficult. Depending on the defensive alignment and blocking assignments, the center's responsibility was to cut off either the onside defensive tackle or middle linebacker in a 4-3 defense, or the tackle playing over him in an odd-front scheme.

The center's block was crucial, since the pulling of the guards left the defensive tackle opposite them uncovered for a split second. Unless the center could get into his block and cut off the defensive tackle quickly, the defender would penetrate the backfield and smear the ball carrier for a loss.

The power sweep *was* Lombardi—fundamentally sound, few frills, and men working together as a team. It was the first play Lombardi put in when he took over in Green Bay, telling us, "Gentlemen, if we can make this play work, we can run the football."

It's as basic a play as there can be in football. We made it work with constant drilling, beginning and ending each and every practice session with the power sweep.

Coach Lombardi wanted his players to be able to run this sweep in their sleep. If we called the sweep 20 times, he'd expect it to work 20 times, not 18 or even 19. We did it so often in practice that there was no excuse for screwing it up.

When Green Bay hired Lombardi in 1959, he needed just two years to get the Packers into the championship game and three years to win the first of his record five league championships.

The dynasty had begun, and at the heart of it was the Packers Sweep, Lombardi's signature play.

Chapter  9

A Quarterback Controversy

The 1959 preseason saw the Packers play six preseason games and winning four. We really began to believe in ourselves and were convinced that we could take on anyone in the league. But the *Press-Gazette* had urged fans to be patient and not expect miracles.

We opened the 1959 season on Sunday, September 27, against the Chicago Bears in Green Bay. A crowd of 32,150 packed into City Stadium. The sky was gray, and the field was wet. It was time for Lombardi's off-season trades and signings to prove themselves to the fans.

Vince drafted Colorado quarterback Boyd Dowler and converted him into a flanker; he traded All-Pro end Billy Howton to Cleveland for defensive end Bill Quinlan and defensive tackle Henry Jordan. Completing his list was the acquisition of safety Emlen Tunnell from the Giants and offensive guard Fred "Fuzzy" Thurston in a trade with coach Weeb Ewbank of the Baltimore Colts.

In the locker room, Vince gave us his fire-and-brimstone pregame pep talk, which concluded with, "Now go through that door and bring back a victory!"

Bill Forester got so excited that he slammed his arm against his locker. It would be the worst injury he would receive all year!

By early in the fourth quarter, the Bears were beating us 6–0. We finally pulled it together and scored nine points in the final seven minutes of the fourth quarter to upset Chicago 9–6. Sloshing through the mud, I followed pulling guards Thurston and Kramer on a sweep left from five yards out to give us a 7–6 lead. Next, Jordan and Nate Borden combined to trap Bears quarterback Ed Brown deep in the end zone for a safety, making the score 9–6. Even Nitschke got into the act.

On Chicago's free kick following the safety, the Bears kicked it short, hoping to recover the ball, but Nitschke fell on it, securing the win as we ran out the clock. When the final gun sounded, we triumphantly swept Vince up onto our shoulders. When we arrived to the locker room, Coach shouted, "We're on our way now!"

In our next two games we upset the Lions and the 49ers to lead the league with a 3–0 record. Packers fans were euphoric, but the undefeated record would not last for long.

The following week the Los Angeles Rams annihilated us 45–6. It would be the beginning of a five-game losing streak. We lost 38–21 on the road to Baltimore, 20–3 to the Giants, and 28–17 to Chicago. After a loss, Lombardi was usually surprisingly gentle to the players, but after the Bears game, he completely lost his temper. He screamed at the offense for playing so lackadaisically. That was the first time I ever saw him slam lockers and throw helmets.

Our final loss came at home against Baltimore. The Colts beat us 28–24. After the game, a reporter asked Vince when he predicted the team would win again. Vince said, "I don't know. The way it's going, I don't know. I'll say this much, this club hasn't quit. They've stayed right in there."

As far as the quarterback situation went, it was still unsettled. All three quarterbacks—McHan, Francis, and Starr—had either physical and/or psychological problems with the game—and each was different.

Lamar McHan was the talented veteran who was big and strong but extremely moody. Joe Francis was a great athlete but inexperienced as a quarterback and a poor passer. Bart's problem was lack of confidence and lack of faith in his ability to get the job done.

McHan was at the helm for the opening three victories, but his performance was inconsistent. Lamar was injured in the Giants game, and Francis replaced him. His ineffectiveness lost us the game 20–3. McHan had reinjured himself, and Starr was called upon to lead the Packers against the Bears. Even though we lost 28–17, Bart played a great game.

With Lamar still physically unable to perform, Starr again took the reins and proved himself the following week at home against the Colts.

Bart started the game, and his intense determination brought the Packers back from a 21–3 halftime deficit. He passed to me for 20 yards and a touchdown to cut the Colts' lead to four points.

We ended up losing the game 28–24, but Starr's performance on the gridiron caught Lombardi's eye. Even though McHan was healthy enough to play the ninth game, Vince's intuition told him to go with Starr. Bart was finally coming into his own. Coach said to Bart, "You are going to be our quarterback from here on out. I want you to relax, be calm, and continue studying like you are doing. Don't be concerned about the play of anybody else. Everything else will take care of itself, and we'll win these ballgames."

It was as though Lombardi was psychic.

On November 22, 1959, the losing streak ended when we defeated the Redskins at home 21–0. Bart threw 19 times and completed 11 of those passes. He spotted a weakness in the defense and had the other backs and me running through the big holes.

Four days later we beat the Lions in Detroit 24–17 to even our record to 5–5. Bart's confidence began to shine. He completed 10 of his 15 passes for 169 yards. Three thousand fans greeted us at the airport upon our arrival home.

On December 6 we avenged our 45–6 loss to the Rams back in October by beating Los Angeles 38–20 in their own backyard. Vince told the reporters that he never dreamed that we would win six games.

Bart played his best game on December 13 against San Francisco. Completing 20 of 25 passes for 249 yards and two touchdowns, the Pack defeated the 49ers 36–14. The victory over San Francisco gave Green Bay a 7–5 record—its best since 1944 when the team won six championships under coach Curley Lambeau.

On December 14, 1959, 7,500 fans waited patiently in the freezing rain for our plane to land from our West Coast victory. As each of us disembarked the plane, we received an ovation, but it was Lombardi's appearance that triggered a deafening roar from the fans.

The closing games of the 1959 season had demonstrated how capable the Packers really were. We finished with a 7–5 record to tie for third place in the conference.

At the end of the season Wellington Mara contacted Vince asking him to become the head coach of the Giants. The Packers organization was against Vince leaving our team. We all knew that he longed to return to New York, but in the end he decided to remain with Green Bay. The Packers gave him a $10,000 bonus, compensating him for a great season, and the National Football League voted him Coach of the Year.

Chapter

The Dawn of a New Decade

When training camp opened in 1960, I saw more veterans arrive early than I could remember, and they were in better physical condition. They all knew what to expect and came prepared.

Vince's training regimen remained the same—brutal and demanding. He hustled us through the grueling drills and had us running sprints at the end of each practice, but this time we were ready for it. What a difference a year can make.

The year 1960 was also the year that Pete Rozelle, the former publicist and boy genius with the Rams replaced Bert Bell as commissioner upon Bell's death. Rozelle not only saw the big picture but also looked beyond it. He revamped the NFL from a small office in Philadelphia to a luxury office building on Park Avenue in New York. With that, he hooked up the NFL with the television networks. Now the entire country could see their favorite teams play every Sunday right in their own living rooms. Under

Pete, the players from my era did more to promote the league than ever before.

The beginning of the new decade saw the rise of the American Football League with its eight franchises. The NFL owners saw the AFL as a bush league and turned up their noses at them. This would later prove to be a big mistake.

Chapter  11

Don't Worry About It—
It's Just Nitschke

For Ray Nitschke, however, there was little difference between the 1959 and 1960 seasons. Even though the Packers were victorious during all six of their exhibition games, Ray was still confined largely to special teams. He had arrived at training camp with the intent of taking over the starting job from Bettis, but he had made a greater impression early on during a September practice.

The day was hot and humid, and the skies grew dark, signaling an approaching storm. Because of the intense heat, Lombardi told his players that they could practice without their helmets and shoulder pads.

The equipment was placed on the ground near a 25-foot steel structure that stood between the two practice fields.

Just then, the dark clouds and gusty winds released raindrops onto the field. Nitschke was worried that his shoulder pads would be ruined from the rain and ran back to the base of the steel tower to retrieve them. While putting on his pads, he decided, since he was already there, to put on his helmet.

Just as he finished placing his helmet over his head, a strong gust of wind grabbed hold of the steel tower and knocked it over. Steel scaffolding weighing in excess of 1,000 pounds collapsed on Ray, crushing him to the ground. In the midst of the fall, a steel bolt forced its way through the hard plastic helmet four inches above his left temple. Back in the 1960s, the NFL helmets were constructed of plastic with a web suspension that allowed an inch of space between the head and the top of the helmet. That bolt just missed penetrating Nitschke's skull.

When the tower collapsed, we all went running over to the site.

"Who's that guy on the ground?" Lombardi yelled.

The players dug through the debris.

"It's Nitschke!" Starr shouted.

"Nitschke?" Lombardi said. "Oh, he's all right. Now everybody back to practice."

Chapter

Starr Gets the Call

In the first game of the 1960 regular season, Starr would be the No. 1 quarterback against the Chicago Bears.

In front of a crowd of 32,150, Starr moved the Packers down the field all the way to the 30-yard line, but the march ended there. The Bears held and took the ball over on downs. We were only able to score twice during the entire game—I scored on a one-yard run and Paul scored on a two-yard run. Chicago sealed the game by scoring all of their points in the fourth quarter to beat us 17–14.

Lombardi called on Lamar McHan to quarterback the Packers in our second game of the season, against the Detroit Lions.

Under McHan, the Packers were ineffective. Finally Lombardi told Starr to get in there and move the team. That's exactly what he did. Bart did a brilliant job of directing the team down the field. He sent me through the middle of the Detroit line for one touchdown, sent Paul Hornung off-tackle for two more, and sent Tom Moore through on a five-yard run. We ended up whipping the Lions by a score of 28–9.

Lombardi still had yet to be convinced of who would be the permanent No. 1 quarterback.

The third game of the season saw us against quarterback great Johnny Unitas and the world champion Baltimore Colts. Once again, Lombardi pulled out Lamar early in the game and replaced him with Bart.

Starr commanded our team to victory by beating the great Unitas and his Colts 35–21. In that game I scored three touchdowns on a 12-yard, a three-yard, and a one-yard run. Tom Moore scored on a 12-yard pass, and McHan found his way to the end zone after a 35-yard run.

On October 23, 1960, we played the San Francisco 49ers. Hornung was basically a one-man show. He gained 72 yards rushing in 13 attempts and scored two touchdowns on the ground, completed one pass for 20 yards, and caught another for 10. He kicked two field goals, including a personal longest 47-yarder, and tacked on five extra points. Moore also added two more TDs to his career, while Max McGee scored six points on a 12-yard pass. Final score. Hornung and the Packers 41, 49ers 14.

Our next game was against the Steelers in Pittsburgh. It was after this game that Lombardi would make a crucial decision regarding our quarterback problem. Even though Bart had been successful at the end of the 1959 season, Vince still questioned his leadership and effectiveness.

Lamar was a brash and assertive kind of guy but apparently had convinced Vince to start him in the next game. Even though we had won three consecutive games under McHan, his passing was unimpressive.

Throughout the first half of the Pittsburgh game we were struggling on offense, and Lombardi decided to go with Bart in the second half.

Down by a point late in the final quarter, Starr sprung the trap on the Steelers secondary by duping the defenders in on short throws to Knafelc. Bart later sent Boyd Dowler down the middle on a deep post pattern, and I sealed it with a one-yard dive into the end zone with 63 seconds left in the game. The 19–13 win gave us four wins in a row and first place in the West.

On the plane back to Green Bay, everyone was in a celebrative mood… well, almost everyone. McHan was very upset about being pulled at the end of the half. His frustration led him to confront Knafelc with, "You never catch my passes the way you did today for Bart."

Knafelc snapped back, "That's because you never throw me the ball!"

McHan then turned on his roommate Boyd Dowler and said, "You didn't catch my passes, either!"

Boyd didn't answer.

But McHan was not yet through venting his anger. In a restaurant where the players stopped to eat, Lamar stormed into a separate room, where Lombardi was dining with members of the Packers executive board.

As McHan gruffly addressed Vince, he managed to articulate the word *dago* into his spiel. Without knowing it, Lamar had sealed his fate with the team. Five months later and after only two seasons with the Pack, Lamar McHan was traded to the Colts.

The victory over the Steelers led Vince to resolve his quarterback dilemma once and for all. Before the team meeting the following morning, he called Bart to his office. He said, "Your performance in the Chicago game led me to believe we had to make a change. That's why I went with McHan. I haven't been all that happy with his performances either, but stayed with him because we were winning. After the way you brought us back yesterday, however, you're my quarterback, and I'm not changing again!"

Our next game was once again against the Baltimore Colts, but this time we were playing on their home turf. Lombardi had met with the press earlier that week and was quoted as saying, "If the first humans were produced by thunder and lightning, as the Winnebago Indian tradition states, the same is being said of my Packers. Thunder is Jim Taylor, my bruising fullback, on his way to his first thousand-yard season, and Lightning is Paul Hornung, my left halfback, who has an uncanny knack for finding the end zone and lighting up the scoreboard on his way to a record-shattering 176 points. Taylor and Horning are about results, nothing more. Other backfields around the league may be bigger and faster, but none produce like Thunder and Lightning. Taylor loves contact so much that if no defensive back is in his way, he will go and find one. To watch Hornung running at midfield may be nothing special, but near the goal line he is the best."

The old man could be gruff and unrelenting at times, but here he showed another side to him—one that Paul and I will never forget.

On Sunday, November 6, 1960, we played the Colts at Baltimore's Memorial Stadium. I always enjoyed playing Baltimore because we both were fairly equal in talent. They had seven future Hall of Fame members on their team: Raymond Berry, Art Donovan, John Mackey, Gino Marchetti, Lenny Moore, Jim Parker, and Johnny Unitas—not to mention their coach, Weeb Ewbank. We weren't doing too bad ourselves. Our future HOF members numbered eight: Willie Davis, Forrest Gregg, Paul Hornung, Henry Jordan, Ray Nitschke, Jim Ringo, Bart Starr, Willie Wood, and me, and we were coached by Vince Lombardi.

That day Unitas and Starr exhibited an incredible passing duel. Hornung had another outstanding game, and I scored a touchdown on a four-yard run, but when the final gun sounded, the score was Baltimore 38, Green Bay 24.

After our loss to the Colts, more than 2,500 fans awaited our arrival in Green Bay. Coach Lombardi said to them, "I am very proud of a very great performance, both offensively and defensively. We got beat on plays because of inexperienced personnel, but I don't want this to be taken as an excuse."

He went on to praise Bart's 23-for-32, 259-yard effort, but I'm sure he wasn't happy with the four interceptions that Starr had thrown.

Chapter

The Rookie—Willie Wood

After our loss to the Colts, Lombardi showed a bit of empathy toward our inexperienced rookie and future Hall of Fame player, Willie Wood. Willie played defensive back for USC but was not drafted by the NFL. In 1960 he came to the Packers as a free agent and tried out for the team. Lombardi liked what he saw and signed him.

During pregame warm-ups cornerback Jesse Whittenton pulled a leg muscle. A graduate of Texas Western, it was Jesse's fifth professional season with the Packers. Our defensive coach, Norb Hecker, nicknamed his Lone Star backfield—which was made up of Whittenton, Hank Gremminger, and Johnny Symank—the Katzenjammer Kids.

In the middle of the first half, Whittenton tried to cover Raymond Berry but ended up limping off the field in great pain. Lombardi told Hecker to replace Jesse with rookie safety Willie Wood. Wood had never played corner before, but when Norb asked him if he could handle the position, Willie said he could and sprinted onto the field. As soon as he arrived to the huddle, shouts of "No. 24, No. 24" arose from the Colts' bench, signaling Unitas that an untested rookie was in the game. Wood had been burned all day by the aerial combination of Unitas and Berry. Berry finished the day with 10 catches for 137 yards.

At the end of the game and while waiting around at the airport for our flight, Willie Davis and Jim Ringo began telling Wood that he had better prepare to return to his hometown of Washington, D.C., in anticipation of Lombardi's wrath for his poor showing against Baltimore.

Lombardi overheard the guys needling Willie. Vince had an uncanny way of assessing talent and seeing into a player's psyche. It was part of his genius. Vince took Willie aside and said, "Don't you believe anything those fellas say! You're not going anywhere. You're staying right here with me. Every one of those guys making fun of you has had the same thing happen to them. You're going to be here a long as I'm here."

And he was.

Ray Nitschke, the Death of Jack Vainisi, and Linebacker Bill George

On Sunday, November 13, 1960, with a 4–2 record, we played the Cowboys at home and completely annihilated them by a score of 41–7. I had a great game with three touchdown runs—28 yards, 4 yards, and 23 yards. Even Nitschke got into the act with a 43-yard interception return for a touchdown.

The following week we lost to the Rams at home by a score of 33–31. I never found the end zone that day. Hornung ended up with two rushing TDs, and both Moore and Dowler had one each. Lombardi was fuming and told the press, "We didn't come here to play football. It was evident all week long in practice!"

We trailed the Colts by one game with only four remaining in the season, and this was before the wild card had become part of the game.

The only player who seemed to have benefitted from the loss to the Rams was Ray Nitschke. After playing seven weeks of the regular season as

I am Roy Rogers. It was always fun to be a cowboy and ride the pony! Photo courtesy of the author.

Alice and Clark Taylor Sr. and sons. Clark Jr. is on the left, I'm on the right, and Webb is on Dad's lap. Photo courtesy of the author.

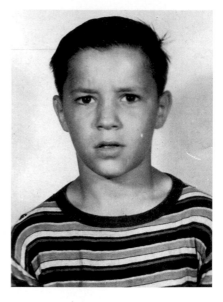

School Days 1945–46.
My fifth-grade picture.
Photo courtesy of the author.

All suited up to play in the All-Star Game my senior year in high school. I was a first-team All-American that year! Photo courtesy of the author.

Here I am stepping on and over teammates and the opposition as I gain yards for the Pack in the first quarter against the Chicago Bears in Chicago on November 8, 1959. Photo courtesy of AP Images.

The Steelers can't bring me down in this early 1960s game. Photo courtesy of Getty Images.

Muddy but unbowed after one hard-fought Packers victory in the early 1960s.
Photo courtesy of Getty Images.

I look like a berserker running with the ball in this 1961 game against the Vikings.
Photo courtesy of Getty Images.

I led the team to a 49–17 victory over the Cleveland Browns in this October 15, 1961, game as I repeatedly exploited the holes in their defensive line. Photo courtesy of Getty Images.

Sam Huff puts a bear hug on me during this September 4, 1962, game. Despite their best efforts, however, we went on to beat the Giants 20–17. Photo courtesy of AP Images.

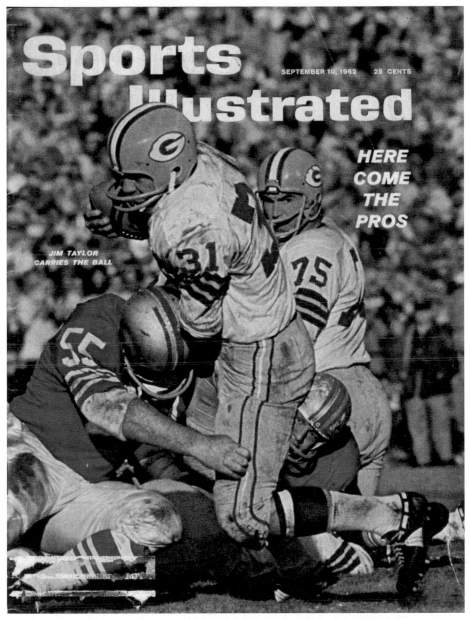

Sports Illustrated

SEPTEMBER 10, 1962   25 CENTS

HERE
COME
THE
PROS

JIM TAYLOR
CARRIES THE BALL

My first Sports Illustrated *cover—September 10, 1962.* Photo courtesy of the author.

My teammate Ron Kramer (No. 88) raises his hands in jubilation as I run into the end zone for a touchdown in the second quarter of the 1962 NFL Championship Game at Yankee Stadium in New York on December 30, 1962. Photo courtesy of AP Images.

My son Chip, shown here at age 2 in 1964, loved to go everywhere with me. Photo courtesy of the author.

a backup to Bettis, he impressed both Lombardi and Coach Bengston with his aggressiveness and toughness. Both coaches decided that a change in the linebacker position was in order.

Our next game was the annual Thanksgiving Day meeting in Detroit against the Lions. During practice that week before the Thursday game, Lombardi told Ray that the starting middle linebacker job was now his. This was definitely a turning point in Nitschke's career.

But even with Nitschke starting at the middle linebacker position, Week 9 saw us lose 23–10 at the hands of the Detroit Lions. Paul ended up scoring all of our points in the fourth quarter. Lombardi was at his wits' end and dejectedly informed the media, "With a 5–4 record, I guess you'd have to say we're out of it."

Even though Lombardi had resigned himself to a disappointing year, he decided to use some reverse psychology on his team. Instead of chewing us out for our loss to Detroit, he let us drink liquor on the flight home, spoke of how we would turn the remainder of the season into a positive, and upon arriving in Green Bay, took us and our families out to a Thanksgiving dinner at the Elks Club.

On the Sunday after Thanksgiving, Jack Vainisi, the genius behind the Packers draft, collapsed in the bathroom of his home and died at the age of 33 from a chronic rheumatic condition that had swelled his heart to twice its normal size. In his passing, Jack left behind one of the most extraordinary yet underappreciated careers in professional football.

It was Vainisi who strongly recommended that the Green Bay executive board hire Lombardi, and it was Vainisi who scouted and recommended drafting the majority of the players on the 1960 team. Sadly enough, he died before he could see the team that he had built play in their first championship game.

On December 4, 1960, we met the Bears in Chicago for a must-win game. The Packers-Bears rivalry dated back to 1921, and Green Bay hadn't won a game at Wrigley Field since 1952. But once we stepped out onto the field and the adrenaline began to flow, the Bears never had a chance.

We ended up beating them 41–13 with Hornung scoring two touchdowns, two field goals, and five extra points for a total of 23 points and a grand total of 152 points in 10 games for a new NFL record. I ran for 140 yards in 24 carries. Max McGee and I each scored a TD, while Willie Davis blocked a punt and recovered it in the end zone for six. Bart Starr had a great game. He hit on 17 of 23 passes for 227 yards and two TDs. But up until this game, Bart's teammates still held some suspicions that he may be a little short of guts. The Bears game destroyed those fears.

Early in the first quarter Bears middle linebacker Bill George blitzed and flattened Starr with a cheap shot to the mouth, splitting his lip all the way up to his nose. With blood streaming down his face, Bart looked up at George, who didn't even offer his hand to help him up to his feet. As Bill started back to the Bears' huddle, he stopped and turned to look at Bart and said, "I'll take care of you, Starr! You're a pussycat!"

As Starr rose to the occasion—spitting blood—he delivered an intense array of cuss words and expletives directed right at Bill. I think that was the first and only time I ever heard Bart swear as he sized up the rugged linebacker.

Bart returned to the huddle without saying another word. He just directed the next play right at Bill George, and the next, and the next. We ran all over the Bears, and no one ever questioned Starr's leadership again.

Hornung, on the other hand, loved to defy authority.

After one of Paul's scores, the Chicago fans in the end-zone stands began chanting, "Throw the ball! Throw the ball!" So naturally, Hornung did.

Bears coach George Halas wasn't amused by Paul's antics and yelled out to him that he owed Chicago $25 to cover the cost of the ball. Paul just smiled and ignored the threat. By the way, he never did pay him.

Hornung really enjoyed playing against Halas. He respected Papa Bear and loved it when Coach would cuss him out from the sideline. Paul used to get into a stance on Halas' side of the field and conspicuously lean to the left. He would hear Halas yell at his players, "Watch Hornung! Watch Hornung! He's going left!" But on the snap, Paul would cut to the right, and Halas would go nuts.

Meanwhile, in the clubhouse Lombardi was all smiles. He said, "We played a real good game, but now we have to hope Detroit can beat Baltimore today. Does anyone know the score?"

One of the reporters had said that Baltimore was leading 15–13 with less than a minute to go. You could see Lombardi wince. "We have to hope that someone beats the Colts or we're out of it," he said.

Just then one of the sports reporters came running into the room. Out of breath, he shouted, "The Lions scored on the last play of the game and beat the Colts 20–15!"

Chapter

Setting Our Sights on the Championship

Lombardi was overjoyed but knew that both the Packers and the Colts still had two games left—both on the West Coast and both against the same two clubs—the San Francisco 49ers and the Los Angeles Rams.

On December 10, 1960, we shut out the 49ers at Kezar Stadium by a score of 13–0. We were favored to win the game but didn't count on it to rain, leaving the field in swamplike conditions. Paul and I together trudged through the mud until Paul finally scored a touchdown and then set up two field goals. That same weekend the Colts had lost 10–3 to Los Angeles, which left us in sole possession of the West by a game over both Baltimore and San Francisco.

The following week we were scheduled to play the Rams at the L.A. Coliseum. It all came down to this one game and a chance to win our first title since 1944. We were all a little nervous but none more than Bart. He and his roommate, Gary Knafelc, were up at 5:30 AM. Leaving the pregame meal early, they both decided to take a walk along the Santa Monica

Beach to ease their nerves. Because they left early, they failed to hear the announcement that the team bus would be leaving at 10:15 instead of 10:30.

I used to do this little thing to coach that would drive him crazy. I would loiter around the side of the bus until the last possible second just to watch him get teed off.

I was doing just that when Bart and Gary finally showed up. Good thing they both stayed on Lombardi time, arriving at the bus seven minutes before departure. With the championship on the line, this was not the time to raise a man's blood pressure. "This is going to cost you two a bundle!" Lombardi said as he blocked the doorway of the loaded bus while pointing his finger at both Bart and Gary.

Luckily for both of them, we blew away the Rams 35–21 and Lombardi told them to forget the $50 fine.

When our plane landed in Green Bay 15,000 cheering fans were waiting in subfreezing weather.

Later that evening we all went to Speed's, one of our popular hangouts. The place was overfilled with screaming fans. There were more than 300 people celebrating our win. Bill Quinlan and Willie Davis were shouting, "We'll win the title! We'll beat the Eagles!"

At the end of the Rams game, I was informed that I had just tied Jim Brown for the league rushing title. In a celebratory mood while consuming champagne at Speed's, I got everyone's attention and made an announcement: "Look, the team with heart is going to win it. We've got heart. We're going to be the champions of the National Football League. We never gave up hope and wanted to win right from the start. How about that!"

Shouting and chanting echoed throughout the bar.

I really believed—as did my teammates—that we could beat the Eagles. We knew we could run on them and move the ball however and whenever we wanted. Our only concern was stopping their quarterback, Norm Van Brocklin.

Chapter

The 1960 Championship Game: Green Bay at Philadelphia, December 26, 1960

Since the weather in Green Bay was below zero and the field was frozen solid, we didn't get in a lot of field practice. On Christmas Eve, we flew to Philadelphia, where we found the weather to be much the same. On Christmas Day we had a brief workout, then returned to our hotel rooms to prepare ourselves for the next day's game.

Unexpectedly, we awoke the following morning to warm and unseasonably comfortable weather conditions as we geared up to play the Eagles for the 1960 NFL championship at Franklin Field in the City of Brotherly Love. The warm weather thawed out the frozen field and turned the gridiron into a slick and muddy mess.

It would be the last playoff game for Norm Van Brocklin and the first for Vince Lombardi as a head coach.

The Eagles had a veteran team led by iron man Chuck Bednarik, who played center on offense and linebacker on defense—the last of the 60-minute men. They also had a great veteran quarterback in Norm Van Brocklin. Philadelphia was considered the underdog, but the 67,325 screaming Philly fans didn't seem to agree with the consensus.

It turned out to be one hell of a game.

In the first quarter, Nitschke eluded a Bednarik block and slammed halfback Ted Dean so ferociously that he forced a fumble, and outside linebacker Bill Forester recovered for the Packers. Paul kicked one field goal in the first quarter and a second in the second quarter to give us a 6–0 lead. But the lead didn't last long. The Dutchman, Van Brocklin, hit Tommy McDonald for a 35-yard TD pass, making the score 7–6. The Eagles added another three points to extend their lead to 10–6 while Hornung missed a 13-yard field goal just before the half.

The third quarter was scoreless, but the battle between Nitschke and the Eagles' offense was ongoing throughout the game. Ray and Bednarik went at it all afternoon. But it didn't end there. Eagles receivers also kept a constant eye out for Ray whenever they ran crossing patterns over the middle—a section of turf that Tommy McDonald referred to as "Nitschke territory." He said, "When you went across the middle of him, you better bring your lunch with you. If he could hit you, he was going to hit you. In those days, there was no five-yard limit beyond the line of scrimmage, and if the ball was in the air, you better watch your head."

Early in the fourth quarter the bright lights of Franklin Field had transformed into a ghostly glow as the fog blanketed the cold, hard gridiron. Despite the fog, Starr quickly realized that Max McGee was not being rushed and hit him for a 35-yard gain and a first down on the Eagles' 45. He then hit Hornung on the 20 for another first down. With the ball on the Eagles' 7-yard line, Bart saw McGee slanting toward the end zone. Starr rifled a pass through the fog at Max, hitting him on the goal line as he fell into the end zone for six points. The score was Packers 13, Eagles 10 with less than five minutes left in the game. Time was running out for the Eagles.

The lead was short-lived as Eagles rookie fullback Ted Dean took Hornung's kickoff and returned it to the Packers' 39-yard line. The Eagles showed no mercy as they pounded away at us, allowing Dean to score from the 5, making the score 17–13, Eagles.

With only a minute and a half left in the game, Bart came back and led us on a long drive that seemed to unnerve the Eagles and their fans. With eight seconds left on the clock, we had the ball on the 25-yard line. I caught a short pass from Starr and quickly broke two tackles, but that old SOB Bednarik hit me on the Eagles' 10-yard line. I refused to go down, and for several seconds we battled each other until three other Eagles hit me and we crashed to the ground. Chuck continued to hold me down on the ground as the last few seconds ticked off the clock.

When the final gun sounded, Bednarik stood over me and said, "You can get up! This goddamn game is over!"

Then Bednarik looked up at the roaring stands, lifted his twisted and distorted fists high above his head, and gave a chilling shout of triumph.

As I made my way to my feet, Hornung came over to me. Injured and shrouded in a warm-up cape, we began to walk off the field together. Just then Bednarik stepped between us and embraced both Paul and me. He told us that we had a hell of a football team and would be back in the championship next year.

Robert Riger took a famous photo of the three of us from behind as we walked off the battlefield arm-in-arm, exhausted and limping.

Everyone, of course, had taken the loss badly, but it was Nitschke who took it the hardest—especially after listening to the comments that Van Brocklin had made to the press while celebrating in the Eagles' locker room. He said, "The Packers' middle linebacker Ray Nitschke had been out of position at times, allowing the Eagles to create big plays."

Ray had prepared himself for the game as well as he could and believed that he was getting blamed for the loss. He was aware that his aggressiveness caused him to make a few mistakes but not enough to deem him the cause of the loss.

In the days that followed, Lombardi would shield his players from the blunt of the blame by informing the press that the loss wasn't just the fault of the team. Coaching errors had also been made. Ray appreciated the public stance that Lombardi took.

In the locker room after the Eagles game had ended, Vince gave one of his better speeches: "I am very proud of all of you, and you have all played well enough to win this game but were beaten by a veteran quarterback who happened to have a great day. I'm sure that there is no doubt in your minds now, and that's why you will win it all next year. This will never happen again. You will never lose another championship!"

And he was right.

Chapter  17

Road to the World Championship

In late March 1961, what remained of the "quarterback controversy" was officially over. Lombardi had traded Lamar McHan to the Baltimore Colts and there was no doubt that Bart was our No. 1 quarterback.

Lombardi told the press, "Starr is my No. 1 quarterback. We rise or fall with him."

Bart met with the sportswriters at the 1961 summer camp and said, "The trade really gave me the confidence I needed. I know that the coach is willing to go with me alone. Things haven't bothered me the way they used to. Some years ago, if I threw an interception, even here at camp, I'd brood about it. Or if I made a bad call, I'd let it bother me, and that only makes things worse. Now, after an interception or a bad call, I forget them. But I know I'd better rectify my mistake…and quick!"

Green Bay was ecstatic with the anticipation of the 1961 season. The NFL had expanded. The Minnesota Vikings, coached by newly retired Eagles quarterback Norm Van Brocklin, were now the new kids on the block. The NFL season would now see each team play 14 rather than 12 league games.

It was also a time of negotiating new contracts. Lombardi had a knack for avoiding arguments with his players and would prevent their efforts by any means necessary. The players' union had yet to become a bargaining force. Agents were unheard of, and players had minimum freedom and even less security.

When Bob Skoronski made his case for a raise, Lombardi quickly pulled out his stats and said, "You had a pretty good year, but against the Rams we had a third-and-one and we ran a 36, and you didn't get the job done, did you, Bob?"

Skoronski countered by referring to a decisive block he had made against San Francisco. Before he could finish, Lombardi stood up from his desk, walked over to Skoronski, and affectionately rubbed the top of his head. The ploy silenced Skoronski, and the debate was over. Lombardi 1, Skoronski 0.

A similar situation was negotiated with Gary Knafelc. Gary was so nervous about talking to Lombardi about his contract that he took the time to type his accomplishments on a sheet of paper. Remembering what happened, Knafelc said, "I walked in, and he acted like he was on the phone and left me just standing there. I was just perspiring. He looked at me and said, 'Sit down!' I sat down.

"I said, 'Coach, I have this...' He stopped me and said, 'Just a minute.' He had to make another call. I knew I was dead already. He hung up and said, 'Yes?' And I said, 'Please read this. It listed my passes caught to passes thrown, blocking awards, grasping anything I could. He didn't look at it a second and a half and then threw it back to me and with that big finger he had he pointed clear across the table at me and said, 'Gary, all you played was offense. You were not on the kickoff team. You were not on the punt return team. All you played was offense!' He said he would give me $2,000 instead of four. And I got up and left the room. I was so happy just to be invited back to training camp. But that's the kind of guy he was. He would build you up, but never to the point too high where you thought you could tell him what to do. He was still the master, and you were the slave."

At St. Norbert's that summer, Lombardi began a tradition of starting from scratch. He reviewed fundamentals of blocking and tackling, how to read the playbook, and basic plays in general. He would begin training camp with the most elementary statement of all. Holding a pigskin in his right hand, he would say, "Gentlemen, this is a football."

Max McGee would always respond with, "Uh, Coach, could you slow down a little. You're going too fast for us."

That statement made even Lombardi smile, but only for a moment. The intensity of his daily workouts continued. Willie Wood remembers it well. "This guy was full of piss and vinegar from the first day of camp. I mean he was hot! You had to work your tail off. He took no nonsense from anybody. He knew that he had a big challenge, and he was determined not to lose again."

Lombardi made two major changes that year in the starting lineup. He moved Ron Kramer into Gary Knafelc's spot at tight end because he felt that Kramer was bigger and a more ferocious blocker. It also added another dimension to the Packers' offense. Willie Wood ended up replacing Emlen Tunnell at free safety.

Tunnell taught Wood many lessons on playing the position and helped him tremendously. Willie really looked up to him. But on game day, Willie was nervous as hell. His pregame routine in the locker room was to sit by himself at his cubicle and chew on a fresh, white towel. After chewing through the first towel, he would begin on a second towel. And after that, he would walk over to the bathroom and throw up. That seemed to calm him down, because once he stepped foot on the field, he was ready to viciously take on the opposition.

That year Willie and rookie cornerback Herb Adderley added a new dimension to the Packers' punt- and kickoff-return team: the threat of returning both for touchdowns.

The bars in the town of Green Bay outnumbered the churches. Most, if not all, were off limits, but that didn't stop many players from entertaining the thought. Places like Piccadilly, King's X, Cinderella's Glass Slipper, the Spot, Candlestick, Chatterbox, First and Last Club, Harvey and Aileen's, Hanks, Helen's Tiny Tap, Gail's, Buzz Inn, Josie and Murph's, Jerry and Irene's, Howard's, Harold's, Lucille and Whitey's, and Marie and Harv's were only a few of the watering holes frequented by the Packers and intensely looked down upon by Lombardi.

Exhibition games were an important part of Lombardi's philosophy. He felt that a break from training camp was good for his players, so he scheduled games in more obscure places such as Winston-Salem, North Carolina; Columbus, Georgia; and Cedar Rapids, Iowa. His philosophy also included winning those exhibition games because the positive effect of victory would carry over into the regular season.

After sweeping the exhibition season by beating the Cowboys 30–7, the Cardinals 31–10, the Bears 24–14, the Giants 20–17, and the Redskins 31–24, we opened the regular season at home against the Lions. After outscoring the opposition 136–72 in total preseason points, we had high expectations about playing Detroit.

Even the sportswriters were predicting that the Packers would repeat winning their second Western Conference title in two years. Some even foresaw that we would go all the way by winning the 1961 world championship.

On Sunday, September 17, 1961, in County Stadium in Milwaukee and in front of 44,307 fans, we began our road to the championship. It was the largest crowd ever to witness a football game in Wisconsin—and they witnessed a 17–13 upset by the Lions.

Detroit just annihilated our defense and sacked Bart numerous times throughout the afternoon. The Lions broke down our blocking and blitzed our passing game.

Stung by the loss, we came back on September 24 to beat the San Francisco 49ers by a score of 30–10. Then, a week later, we shut out the Bears 24–0. Both games were at home.

On October 8 we crushed the Colts at Lambeau Field. Paul scored four touchdowns, six points after, and a field goal for 33 points—a Packers record and the third-highest single-game total in NFL history.

A week later, on October 15, we played the Browns in Cleveland and just whipped them by a score of 49–17. During that game, Lombardi came up with another of his innovations. He placed a photographer on the roof of Cleveland Stadium. The photographer then used a Polaroid camera to take photos of the opposing team's formations. Upon developing the photos, he would insert them into a weighted sock and then throw them down to the Green Bay bench for Lombardi to review.

By the third quarter, we were far ahead of the Browns, and Starr called a 63, which was a play developed for Hornung. Paul told Bart that he didn't want the ball. He told him, "This is Jim's game, so let him do the scoring."

Bart handed off the ball to me, and I added another six points to the board. At the end of the game, I had outgained Jim Brown 158 yards to his 72 yards and outscored him 24–0.

After the score, I jogged back to the bench and sat down next to Paul. I turned to him, smiled, and said, "Who's Jimmy Brown?"

After the game, Lombardi praised the team and told us, "This was the best game we've ever played!"

Chapter  18

The Running Back Matchup—Taylor vs. Brown

Fans and sportswriters constantly compared Jim Brown and me, even though we were different kinds of runners. Brown ran straight up but had to be tackled low. His breakaway speed was better than mine; therefore he was a greater threat to break off a long run. He had a way of relaxing when opponents had him in their grasp that helped him avoid injuries, and he could lull a tackler into a mistake.

I, on the other hand, ran close to the ground and fought for every inch, putting my strength against the bigger men who tried to bring me down. Each play was a mini war. Sam Huff once said that I would have made a great linebacker.

Brown and I had four face-to-face meetings. In October 1961, the Packers and Browns each led their divisions with 3–1 records when they squared off at Cleveland. Green Bay turned what was expected to be a close game into a 49–17 rout, as I ran for 158 yards and scored four touchdowns.

Brown settled for 72 yards as his team was forced to pass once they fell far behind.

In 1962 I beat Brown for the rushing title and was league MVP.

The second meeting hardly counted. In January 1964 at Miami, the Pack beat the Browns 40–23 in the late and unlamented Runner Up Bowl—a showdown between the division second-place finishers concocted by the NFL. I played only the first half and gained 44 yards. Brown ran only 11 times for 56 yards.

A truer test came the following November at Green Bay. I was playing with banged-up ribs, was held to 63 yards in 22 caries compared to Brown's 74 for 20, but I led a second-half comeback that gave the Packers a 28–21 victory over the championship-bound Browns.

The final confrontation was, of course, the 1965 championship game— Brown's last in a Cleveland uniform. Playing on a muddy Green Bay field, Brown was held to 50 yards. I, with 96, was named the game's MVP.

My totals for the four meetings were 361 yards on 83 carries and seven touchdowns. Brown had 252 yards on 59 attempts and a single touchdown. Realistically, the Packers were the stronger team overall, and Cleveland was blown out in three of the four games, severely limiting Brown's running chances.

Chapter 19

President Kennedy and Coach Lombardi vs. the U.S. Army

In 1961 President Kennedy ordered a buildup of the armed forces due to increased tension with the Soviet Union over access to West Berlin. The national guard and reserve units were called upon to serve. This had a great effect on professional football, but the Packers were hit harder than any other team.

The day following our victory over Cleveland, Ray Nitschke, Boyd Dowler, and Paul Hornung were ordered to report for active army duty. The hostilities between the U.S. and the Soviet Union had escalated, forcing the East Germans, who were then controlled by the Russians, to build a concrete and steel structure that would later be known as the Berlin Wall.

To say that Coach Lombardi was really upset about this would be an understatement. He later told the press, "They are doing a good job on us!

You can't lose three starters [Nitschke, Dowler, and Hornung] and keep winning!"

All of a sudden it was made known that Paul had a pinched nerve in his neck. It didn't stop him from playing football, but it did cast doubt on his army duties. His call-up was deferred until the nerve could be examined. In the meantime he continued to play football. It looked as though Hornung was receiving preferential treatment, and he was.

In October 1961, Wisconsin's U.S. Senator Alexander Wiley requested that the Department of Defense defer both Hornung and Nitschke until the season had concluded. He unleashed a storm of protests from citizens, media, and political colleagues.

With that, Lombardi's protests fell on deaf ears. Hornung decided to do the right thing. He quickly went through his physical, passed it, and reported for duty at Fort Riley, Kansas, as a radio operator and jeep driver. As for Nitschke and Dowler, they reported to Fort Lewis, Washington.

In reality though, the NFL was still receiving preferential treatment. Dowler and Nitschke were both granted weekend passes and played in every game. Hornung missed only two.

Finally, enough was enough. Lombardi called his friend in Washington, D.C., who was well connected with President Kennedy's military advisor. Coach told the media, "Through an arrangement, we were able to get those three players released for playing on Sunday. The Kennedy administration cooperated unbelievably with us."

Los Angeles sports columnist Jim Murray was quoted as jokingly saying, "The Green Bay Packers may be the first team ever to win the Cold War and the National League championship in the same year. In an emergency though, the Packers run the risk of losing good soldier Hornung. If there's an alert, he'll have to get back to that jeep in Kansas and turn the radio off."

But for Lombardi, this was no laughing matter. The fact that his three starters couldn't practice with the team disrupted routine, not to mention the coordinating of plays.

Even with the world—and the Packers—in crisis, Green Bay went on to prevail. We beat the Vikings both at home and away, 33–7 and 28–10, respectively. But we lost 45–21 to the Colts in Baltimore. In Chicago we just squeezed by the Bears 31–28, ran over the Rams 35–17 at home, beat the Lions 17–9 in Detroit, and won our final regular-season home game 20–17 against the Giants. Our record was 10–2 with only the 49ers and Rams left to play away.

Prior to the beginning of the San Francisco game, Lombardi left the team alone in the locker room to discuss whatever it was they wanted to say. Jim Ringo was our center and team captain. He asked if there was anything anyone wanted to say before we went out on the field. Paul, never at a loss for words, stepped forth and addressed the team in typical Hornung style: "Guys, there are three of us here from the service—me, Nitschke, and Boydie. And we're real happy to be here, and we needed this weekend a helluva lot more than you guys. And I want to tell you something. I came here for two things. I took care of the first one last night; now, let's take care of the second and kick the 49ers' *ass!!*"

The team just lost it. Our laughter was so loud that Lombardi was able to hear it outside the locker room. He always wanted his players to be totally serious before a big game and was not amused by the hysterics that illuminated the locker room and Kezar Stadium tunnel.

"What's so funny?" shouted Lombardi.

Paul answered him with a smile and said, "Coach, we're just laughing about how we're going to celebrate after we win this damned game!"

But the last laugh was on us, as the 49ers beat us by one point, 22–21.

The following week we defeated the Rams 24–17 minus Hornung, because he had to return to Fort Riley, and won the Western Division title with an 11–3 record. We were the best in the league.

The stage was set to play the New York Giants for the championship in the first-ever playoff game to be held in Green Bay. But there was still one problem that needed to be resolved: Hornung's captain would not allow Paul to leave for the game.

He was supposed to begin a six-day leave the Tuesday following the championship game. He asked his captain if he could switch the leave to December 27 through January 3 so he would be able to play in the NFL title game. Much to his surprise, the captain said no.

Paul immediately called Lombardi and told him there was a problem. He listened, then said, "Let me make a phone call, and I'll call you back in 20 minutes."

When Lombardi called back, he said, "I think your captain is about ready to get a phone call that will get you off to play."

Coach had called President Kennedy. The captain immediately received a call from the White House. When he heard the voice on the other end of the line say it was President Kennedy in that Bostonian accent of his, he thought the call was a joke and responded with, "Yeah, and this is Donald Duck." But when the unimaginable became a reality and he realized that it was really Kennedy, it wasn't long before Paul was on his way to Green Bay to play in the championship on December 31.

The 1961 Championship Game: New York at Green Bay, December 31, 1961

In the Packers locker room on the final day of 1961, players sat around killing time before the start of the NFL Championship Game. Max McGee was in his usual comical mood and said, "Everybody look pretty. There's gonna be 20 million people watching us on TV."

"How many of them are female?" asked a teammate.

"Maybe 5 million," said Max. "And the Horn knows half of them!"

Private First Class Paul Hornung, on leave from Fort Riley Kansas, just shook his head and smiled.

The 1961 championship game against New York was the first NFL playoff game ever held in Green Bay. CBS sent their No. 1 team, Lindsey Nelson and Chris Schenkel, to broadcast the event on TV.

The entire town of Green Bay prepared to host the title game. They had waited 17 years for this. The name Titletown, U.S.A. was officially

73

designated by the chamber of commerce. "Welcome to Titletown" was the first message the Giants received upon arriving in Green Bay. Even the Milwaukee railroads got involved in the celebration. They brought in special trains to take fans to Green Bay. Eighty police officers were brought in to keep the peace just in case anything happened. All phone calls at St. Norbert College were answered with, "Beat the Giants." This phone-answering craze soon swept throughout the Green Bay region. Even the desk clerk at the hotel where the Giants were staying made sure to give a cheerful, "Howdy, Packer-Backer wake-up call" to each and every Giants player on the morning of game day.

On December 31, the temperature at City Stadium was 20 degrees and clear. There was an 11-mph wind coming in from the northwest. The stadium's field was clean but frozen. A tarp was laid across the entire gridiron and held down by 20 tons of hay—not to mention 14 inches of snow, but it would still be hard for Packers and Giants runners to cut. More than 39,000 bundled-up fans crowded themselves into the stadium. It was anticipated that 41,000 would be attending, but by game time, more than 1,000 tickets still remained unsold.

As the Packers came out onto the field, the sun suddenly broke through the clouds. It proved to be an omen of how the afternoon's game would develop. Throughout the day, both sidelines were afforded warmth by gas heaters that reflected heat off a concave structure behind the players and bounced onto our bodies.

But during pregame warm-ups, both Hornung and I decided to play with the Giants' psyche a little. We came out on the field in the freezing cold with just our T-shirts. New York was freezing their rear ends off while we ran around as if we were on the sunny beaches of Hawaii. We were basically telling them that this was our kind of weather—Packers weather—and we were ready to play ball.

New York was an arrogant yet confident team. Players like Sam Huff were convinced that the Giants would easily defeat this Midwestern ballclub.

Their offense consisted of quarterback Y.A. Tittle; wide receiver Del Shofner; running backs Alex Webster, Phil King, and Joel Wells; receivers Joe Walton and Kyle Rote; and a tough offensive line made up of Rosey Brown, Jack Stroud, Ray Wietecha, and Darrell Dess.

The New York defense was defined by linebacker Sam Huff and defensive ends Andy Robustelli and Jim Katcavage. The Giants' tackles were Dick Modzelewski and Rosey Grier. They were the first defensive line to earn the nickname the Fearsome Foursome—and they definitely earned their name.

With both team captains on the field, the game was ready to begin. The Giants won the coin toss and elected to receive. Ben Agajanian, backup kicker to Hornung, kicked off, and Joel Wells returned the ball to the Giants' 30-yard line.

As a record-breaking 55 million viewers watched the game on television, the Packers came as close to perfection as Lombardi could ever take them.

Early in the first quarter, Tittle threw a deep ball to Kyle Rote at the Packers' 10. Rote dropped the pass, and the Giants' best opportunity of the game had literally slipped through their fingers. After a scoreless first quarter, the Packers finally scored on the first play of the second quarter.

The second quarter began with a six-yard TD run by Hornung. Moments later, Henry Jordan stretched his fingers out to tip a Tittle pass into the hands of Ray Nitschke. The interception set up Green Bay at the New York 33. Next, Bart passed to Ron Kramer for 16 yards, and I ran for four to the Giants' 13. From there Starr passed to Boyd Dowler for six more points. We were ahead 14–0.

Green Bay was hot and ready to trounce all over the Giants. Hank Gremminger intercepted a Tittle pass at midfield and returned it to the New York 36-yard line. Next, Paul and I combined and ran the ball down to the 14, and then Kramer caught a pass over the middle from Starr for a third touchdown. This made the score 21–0, with Hornung having kicked all three PATs. The Giants figured that now was the time to put Charlie Conerly in for Tittle. Conerly threw a 35-yard pass to Rote, setting the Giants up deep in Packers territory, but once again, the Giants came away scoreless.

Near the end of the second quarter, Paul rushed for 17 yards and Starr connected with Kramer on a 40-yard pass that highlighted a drive and sent the Packers to the Giants' 15-yard line. A New York offside penalty put the ball on the 10, and Hornung kicked his first field goal of the game for a 24-point quarter.

Kramer played one of his best games ever. He was all over Sam Huff that day. Sam had become an insignificant force for the Giants defense. Besides, we got tired of hearing Chris Schenkel and the media talking about Huff as if he were the greatest linebacker who ever played the game. Hornung went so far as to say that Huff couldn't carry Ray Nitschke's jockstrap.

The Giants were playing their same flex defense, but we matched up better against them. We didn't make mistakes, and they couldn't stop the sweep. There was no denying that the Pack had outplayed and outclassed the Giants in every aspect of the game.

Giants tackle Greg Larson said, following the end of the first half, "When we got behind like that, the Green Bay defensive line dared us to run. They knew we had to pass to catch up. They came in swinging from the heels, with fists and forearms and elbows. It was the most awesome thing I've ever been involved in. We had no way to stop them. They were like wild men. It was unending, it seemed. They constantly punished us."

During the half, the locker room quickly filled up with smoke as Lombardi gave his halftime spiel. Hornung had his usual two Marlboros, Lombardi smoked his Salem cigarettes, Henry Jordan grabbed a Camel from Phil Bengtson, and I pulled out my cigar. The only guy who didn't smoke was Starr.

As the second half began, the Packers came out of the locker room ready to fight. Relentlessly, we continued to annihilate the Giants.

Joe Morrison fumbled away a punt at the Giants' 21. From there Hornung scored his second field goal of the day. Following a 43-yard Packers drive, Starr delivered a 13-yard touchdown pass to Kramer. The Giants came back by getting the ball past midfield for the third and last time, but Tittle was sacked for a 10-yard loss on fourth down, which ended the Giants' final chance to get on the scoreboard.

Soon after, Jesse Whittenton caught Green Bay's third interception of the day at the Packers' 38. I ran for 33 yards on a draw play and spearheaded a drive that ended at the New York 12-yard line. Hornung kicked his 17th, 18th, and 19th point of the game on a 19-yard field goal. The kick set a record for points by a single player in a title game, and there was nothing left to do but run out the clock and celebrate.

With the final seconds of the game ticking down, Herb Adderley intercepted Tittle and returned the ball 14 yards to end the game. Final score:
Packers 37, Giants 0.

The Packers' shutout was the first in a title game since 1949 and the fifth
in 29 games to that point. The Giants had minus-four rushing yards in the
second half and only 50 passing yards in the same two quarters. Due to
the fact that I came into the game with a back injury, the Packers turned to
Hornung to fill their power-running needs.

We outscored, outrushed, outpassed, and outplayed the Giants: We ran
63 plays to New York's 43. We rushed for 181 yards to the Giants' 31. Starr
passed for 164 yards to Tittle's 65. We made 19 first downs compared to the
Giants' six, intercepted four of Tittle's passes and caused a fumble recovery,
and never once turned the ball over to New York.

Paul ended the day with 89 yards rushing and scored a total of 19 points.
And all this with only five days of practice! He also ended up winning the
game MVP award and the new Corvette. He'd already won the season's
MVP award. Lombardi gave the players' wives their own reward for the
victory. He bought a mink stole for each and every one of them!

The game ended at 3:28, at which point the steel goalposts were taken
down by the Packers' fans and paraded up and down the streets of Green
Bay.

In the locker room, Lombardi told us that we were the greatest team in
the history of the National Football League. While in the locker room, the
phone rang. It was for Lombardi. He picked up the receiver of his red tele-
phone, and it was President Kennedy on the other end. He called to offer
his congratulations. Later that day a telegram arrived for Lombardi. It, too,
was from President Kennedy. It read, "Congratulations on a great game. It
was a fine victory for a great coach, a great team, a great town. Best regards,
President Kennedy."

Giants quarterback Tittle addressed the press after the horrific loss,
saying, "We couldn't have beaten them if we had used 22 men at once!"

Lombardi added, "The most important thing about our game was that
the defense kept getting the ball for us. Another thing, before the game, we
tested the ground, and our fellows found they could dig in fairly well with
cleats. Sneakers tended to slip.

"The players did it. They played a hell of a game. No, we didn't expect such a decisive victory. We expected only to win. You people who have followed us throughout the season know we played the same type of game we always play. We ran hard and blocked and tackled hard. There were no gimmicks."

Afterward, Lombardi spoke highly of Paul, saying, "We expected him to play a fine game. He's that type. The greater the competition, the greater he is. We didn't quite know what we were doing last year when we lost to the Eagles. This year we did."

Hornung said, "We knew the Giants would try to stop our weak-side slants, so we used some strong-side stuff—over the middle and to the strong side inside Kramer. It worked beautifully. I told Bart Starr that if we just played our normal game we'd win. We were confident. This is the greatest day in my life."

When it was my turn to address the media, I told them that I wanted the Giants to think I had all my speed. So they keyed on me. Starr kept faking handoffs to me and giving the ball to Hornung, and Paul got through there well.

Giants coach Allie Sherman could not say anything positive about his team. He said, "We didn't even get out the blackboard at halftime. There was nothing to chart, no strategy to discuss. We had been making mistakes, and that was that. You can't pick up dropped passes with a blackboard."

Willie Davis summarized the Packers' attitude coming into the game in two sentences: "It was a personal thing with most of us. We felt that we hadn't been getting the credit and recognition we deserved during the season, neither in the press or the All-Pro selections."

The story had come full circle—the Packers had humiliated the Giants. We had once more become Titletown, USA.

On April 30, 1962, commissioner Pete Rozelle presented Coach Lombardi with the two-foot-high Jim Thorpe Memorial Trophy for winning the NFL championship.

Chapter

1962: A Season to Remember

On the first day of training camp in 1962, a sign was placed above the club-house. It read: "Green Bay Packers—1961 World Champions." On the wall in the clubhouse one of the players had written, "We did it in 1961, we can do it in 1962!"

I remember Coach Lombardi looking around the room and saying, "This is going to be a tough year for us. This season everyone is going to be up to beat us. We won the Western Conference title in 1960, we won it again in 1961. They can't take that away from us. But a lot of people—the Colts, the Bears, the Lions, and the Giants—they are going to try as hard as they can to beat us this season."

He stopped for a moment and stared at us. Then he asked, "Are you going to let them take that title away from us?"

We all shouted, "No!"

With that, we all charged out on to the practice field, mentally and physically ready for the 1962 season. The one thing about Lombardi is that he really got us ready for a game. He constantly repeated himself until we could recognize the opposing team's defenses in our sleep. He gave us the confidence that we needed before facing the challenge.

On July 24, 1962, Paul Hornung was finally discharged from the service and was back with the Packers in time for the August 3 game against the College All-Stars. We, of course, won that game by a score of 42–20.

That same year, Lombardi had made some changes within our offense and defense. In our fifth game of the season, Paul received a knee injury that sidelined him for the remainder of the year. In the meantime, rookie Earl Gros and veterans Tom Moore and Elijah Pitts filled in the backfield when needed, and Jerry Kramer took over the place-kicking position. He ended up booting 38 PATs and nine field goals in 11 attempts. Bart was also injured and ended up throwing only 12 touchdown passes and nine interceptions. The offensive load was now up to me. I ended up with the best year of my career, rushing for 1,474 yards and 19 touchdowns—surpassing Cleveland's Jimmy Brown. Ironically, even with Paul and Bart injured, the Packers had a terrific season.

We totaled over 30 points eight times that season. We outscored our opponents 415–148 and compiled the highest point spread of the postwar era, 19.1 points more than our opponents per game. Our defense was nearly perfect.

Ray Nitschke became a ferocious middle linebacker on the field and a decent individual off the field. That was because he had married Jackie, and she set him straight on how to act. But before then, Nitschke was a wild man. Kramer was not a big fan of Ray's. They had almost come to blows many times in practice and in the locker room. Of Nitschke's and my competitive drives, Kramer said, "Like Jimmy, Nitschke didn't know when to ease up when playing football—didn't know how to 'brother-in-law it'—the Packers term for toning it down against teammates. And he never apologized for his aggressiveness."

He continued, "Ray and Jimmy were alike in their approach to football. Nitschke looked up to Taylor. Just as Nitschke would explain his explosive charge into a running back by saying, 'You want the ball carrier to be a little shy, and a little shyer the next time,' Taylor adopted the same attitude toward defenders.

"Jimmy used to say, 'You've got to sting 'em. If you give a guy a little blast, maybe the next time he won't be so eager.

In practice, both guys often collided in the Packers' nutcracker drill. I remember one occasion when Jimmy was the ball carrier and it was Ray's job to stop him. Nitschke was screened by the blocker, and Taylor ran away untouched. Lombardi immediately stopped the drill and said, 'Mr. Nitschke, I have read that you are the best linebacker in the NFL. But after watching you just then, I find it hard to believe. Now do it again!' On the next play, an irate Nitschke grabbed the blocker by the shoulder pads, lifted him off the ground, and threw him back into Taylor. That pleased Lombardi immensely."

Willie Davis and Henry Jordan were having great years on the front line, as were Herb Adderley at cornerback and Willie Wood at safety. The 1962 season saw Wood intercept nine passes and Adderley seven.

The 1962 Green Bay Packers were definitely a multitalented team.

Our opening game was against the Vikings. This was Minnesota's second year in the league. They were coached by former Eagles quarterback Norm Van Brocklin, and their quarterback (out of Georgia) was Fran Tarkenton. It was also his second year in the league.

In the stands stood 38,000 screaming fans who greeted us with thunderous applause as each Packer was introduced on the field. Within a few minutes, the game was under way.

Green Bay won the toss and elected to receive. On the first play a nervous Bart Starr ran into the huddle and called the play. He took the snap from center Jim Ringo and handed off to me. As the defense charged toward me, I ran for five yards. As I fell to the ground, I took three Vikings with me. I ended up with a total of 17 carries for 75 yards, but it was really Hornung's day to shine.

He and the rest of the team just mowed down the Vikings. Paul scored the first 20 points as we ran over, around, and through the Minnesota defense for a 34–7 victory. Hornung ended up with three touchdowns, three conversions, and two field goals. Our defense intercepted five of Tarkenton's 23 passes.

It may have been an omen, but even before the opening kickoff, defensive end Jim Leo (the first player to be introduced in the pregame ceremonies) slipped and fell on the concrete ramp after his name had been called over the loudspeaker. A few minutes later, after we had won the toss and elected to receive, a strong wind from out of the southwest twice toppled the ball off the tee after place-kicker Mike Mercer had started his approach. Mercer finally had to get a teammate to hold the ball for him.

After our first punt of the game, Minnesota's Bobby Reed fumbled Boyd Dowler's windblown kick and our back, Lew Carpenter, recovered the ball on the Minnesota 7. Two plays later, Hornung crashed into the end zone behind Forrest Gregg.

Minnesota got the ball back but not for long. Tarkenton attempted to throw to end Jerry Reichow, but the throw was off. Instead our linebacker Bill Forester deflected it into the hands of Willie Wood. By halftime, we were winning 17–0.

Bad luck continued for the Vikings as Tarkenton continued to be intercepted and could only find Reichow in the end zone once throughout the entire game. Final score: Packers 34, Vikings 7.

The following week we shut out the St. Louis Cardinals at home by a score of 17–0. Once again we played to a capacity crowd at County Stadium. But by the end of the first half the Cardinals' spread defense and the fact that they held our passing game in check had limited us to three points. Starr then turned to me.

In the second half, Lombardi instructed Bart to forget about the wide stuff and begin running up the middle. To take care of the St. Louis blitz, Green Bay shifted from man-to-man to zone. The shift in tactics proved successful, and I began running into the middle for sizable gains. I charged through the St. Louis defense for 122 of the Packers' rushing total of 171 yards.

On September 30, 1962, we played our third game of the regular season against the Chicago Bears. By then we had won all six of our exhibition games and the opening two. Chicago had just returned from the West Coast and had beaten both the 49ers and the Los Angles Rams. Now it was time for the Pack to play the Bears—the longest-running rivalry in the league. It was George Halas vs. Vince Lombardi, Rick Casares vs. me, Bill George vs. Ray Nitschke, Doug Atkins vs. Willie Davis, and J.C. Caroline vs. Herb Adderley.

The pregame hype never lived up to the expectations of the game. I ended up scoring three touchdowns; Bart, Ron Kramer, and Elijah Pitts each scored one TD apiece; and Adderley returned an interception for six points. Final score: Green Bay 49, Chicago 0.

The following day, the *Chicago Tribune*'s headlines read: "Packers Whip Crippled Bears, 49–0." The subtitles read: "Loss Worst in History of NFL Team. Halas Sums It Up: They Were Too Good for Us."

The *Tribune* also stated:

Fullback Jim Taylor scored three of the touchdowns which went into the largest total Green Bay has scored in the series that has been renewed 86 times in the last 41 years. Taylor went 1 yard for the first one, 3 yards on an identical slant off the Bears' left side for his second, and climaxed one of his better performances by bursting 11 yards through the middle of the Bear line for the third.

Between times, Taylor ran up a total of 126 yards on 17 attempts, 41 more than the entire Bear offense, which obviously had been deprived of its sting through the loss of Willie Galimore and Charley Bivins, and the injury of Rick Casares.

When 255-pound Ron Kramer took in Bart Starr's 54-yard pass for the Packers' second touchdown, it was Taylor who sent J.C. Caroline rising off the turf like a bouncing balloon on the 5-yard line to let the former Michigan All-American get into the end zone.

It was the Packers' fourth consecutive league victory, and with last year's championship playoff and six preseason conquests, including the Chicago All-Star Game, our 11th in a row. Lombardi couldn't have been happier.

On a wet, drizzly October 7, 1962, we played the Lions and were once again at home. The ease with which the Packers beat the Bears was not to be in the game played against Detroit.

We were trailing 7–6 in the fourth quarter with less than two minutes remaining in the game. It was an extremely brutal and physical game, and both teams were completely exhausted. This same team that shut out the Bears only a week before couldn't even find the end zone. If it weren't for Hornung scoring two field goals, we wouldn't have had any points on the board.

Anyway, Detroit had the ball and was in full control—at least that's the way it looked. Then all of a sudden, Lions quarterback Milt Plum threw a pass down and out to his flanker, but his receiver slipped and fell on the muddy turf. The ball soared right into the hands of Herb Adderley, who took it to the Lions' 18-yard line. Two plays later, and with 33 seconds remaining on the clock, Hornung kicked the final field goal that beat Detroit 9–7. Unbelieveable!

After that close call and victory over the Lions, the Pack continued to win. We beat the Vikings 48–21 in Minnesota, but Paul was hit by Vikings linebacker Cliff Livingston and twisted his right knee. He left the game and never returned.

The 49ers came to town on October 21, and I scored two touchdowns, one for 16 yards and a second for 25 yards. I ended the day with 160 yards rushing—improving my six-game rushing total to 742. We beat San Francisco 31–13. Hornung was still sidelined with his knee injury, but Tom Moore started in his spot and Jerry Kramer took over as place-kicker. Little did we know at that time that Paul would be out for the remainder of the season.

On October 28 we played the Colts in Baltimore. Only Ron Kramer and I scored one touchdown apiece while Jerry Kramer kicked two PATs and one field goal. But it was enough to beat Johnny Unitas and his Colts by a score of 17–6. It was our first road win over Baltimore since 1957.

But there was more to this game than just a win over the Colts. Unitas ended up leaving the field with a sprained ankle, and former Green Bay Packers quarterback Lamar McHan took over. He still held a grudge against Lombardi and Starr after being demoted to second-string quarterback and later being traded to Baltimore in 1961.

At the snap, McHan stepped back, looking for a receiver, but our massive defense put a heavy rush on him and he was forced to throw the ball. Unfortunately for Lamar, it landed in the hands of Ray Nitschke, who brought it back 30 yards to the Green Bay 42. Three plays later I exploded through a gaping hole opened up by Jim Ringo and Fuzzy Thurston to rush 37 yards for the game-winning touchdown.

On November 1 we once again faced our nemesis, the Chicago Bears—but this time it was on their turf. But even a home-field advantage didn't help. Once the dust had cleared, the Packers had once more triumphed over Chicago. The headlines of the *Chicago Tribune* read:

"Packers Roll On—And Over Bears 38–7: 48,753 Fans See Taylor Run for 4 Touchdowns."

In the first quarter I rushed for two yards for my first TD. In the third quarter I scored from one yard out—and in the fourth quarter I scored twice on a one-yard run and a two-yard run. Green Bay had now been unbeaten in 16 consecutive ballgames. We once again humiliated the Bears in the wet, 36-degree cold of Wrigley Field. Our record was 8–0.

November 11 saw us playing the Eagles in Philadelphia. Once again I scored four touchdowns for a total of 141 yards rushing, raising my league-leading total to 1,075. The Pack rolled on to nine straight victories and shut out the birds by a score of 49–0. I looked at it as well-deserved payback for the title defeat we endured back in 1960.

We played Baltimore at home on November 18, 1962. It was one of our tougher games. I only rushed for 46 yards, but Adderley ran back a 103-yard kickoff return for six points in the first quarter. Kramer made the PAT and later in that same quarter kicked a 24-yard field goal. In the fourth quarter Tom Moore rushed for a 23-yard score, and again Kramer converted the kick. The defense also held the Colts' offense for two amazing goal-line stands. Final score: Green Bay 17, Colts 13. We had racked up 10 wins and no losses. We began to believe that we were unbeatable.

Chapter

The Turkey Day Massacre

It was the kind of call that turns coaches gray and causes quarterbacks to be traded.

In the fourth game of the 1962 season, the Detroit Lions led the Packers by a score of 7–6. With less than two minutes remaining in the game, I watched from the sideline as Detroit let the clock click down. The first two plays were handoffs that had gained little ground, making it third-and-eight.

Milt Plum, the Lions quarterback, walked over to the sideline to confer with his coach, George Wilson. We all felt that Detroit would call a conservative play—a running play. They probably wouldn't pick up the first down, but the call would use up the clock. The Lions would then have to punt, and the Packers would be forced to cover approximately 70 yards in about 30 seconds. Unfortunately for Detroit, that was not the case.

Plum threw a pass to receiver Terry Barr, who slanted toward the middle of the field, then suddenly cut toward the sideline. On the cut, Barr slipped and fell and Plum's pass zipped right into the arms of Packers cornerback Herb Adderley, who returned the ball 30 yards. With 33 seconds to go in the game, Hornung kicked his third field goal of the day, and we ended up beating the Lions 9–7.

Coach Wilson of Detroit was quoted as saying the following to his team: "That was a tough one out there today. No one hates to lose more than I do. But remember this: the mark of great teams is that they are able to come back. You can't bring that game back, so forget it. Another thing, I called that play, nobody else did. I still think we have the best team in our division and the best quarterback, and we will win this thing."

Wilson was proven wrong. Neither did he have the best team in the NFL West, nor the best quarterback. But out of the ashes of that heartbreaking defeat for Detroit came one of the classic upsets in NFL history.

On November 22 we played the Lions again in their traditional Thanksgiving Day game. By that time, the Packers were hailed as the greatest football team of all time. We had won 10 straight league games and had not been beaten in 18 games. An undefeated year seemed almost inevitable for Coach Lombardi's Big Green Machine.

But that was before Thanksgiving. After the game, we were thankful just to get out of Detroit's Tiger Stadium alive!

Striking relentlessly right from the start, and with a virtually flawless display on both offense and defense, the Lions annihilated us by a score of 26–14. Most consider this the worst loss ever by a Lombardi-coached team.

Bart Starr took the brunt of the beating. Our All-Pro quarterback was savagely attacked by Lions tackles Alex Karras and Roger Brown and ends Sam Williams and Darris McCord. We supposedly had the best offensive line in the league, but Detroit's defensive line hit Starr again and again—rushing past Packers guards Jerry Kramer and Fuzzy Thurston as if they were standing still. Lions linebackers Wayne Walker, Joe Schmidt, and Carl Brettschneider helped sack Starr eight times for losses totaling 76 yards, and that was just in the first half!

The more Bart was hit, the angrier he became. He was always the gentleman—both on and off the field—but even Starr has his limits. He began to blame the officials for the Packers' defeat. He went so far as to take out his anger on referee Red Paice. He told him that he was going to reach out and "bite that big, fat head of his" if he continued to give Green Bay any more of those lousy calls.

Paice stared right into Bart's face and said, "Starr, if you do, you'll be the only quarterback in this league with more brains in his stomach than he has in his head!"

Bart knew right then and there that he had it coming and immediately backed off.

It wasn't just the pass rush alone that held us down. A clever move by the Detroit defensive secondary was extremely successful on our offensive unit.

Usually the pass defenders shift to the strong side—the side where the offensive team positions its wide receiver. But the Lions defenders crossed us up by doubling up on receiver Max McGee even when he was the end of the weak side.

The Lions kept Wayne Walker in front of him and Dick LeBeau behind him as he ran his patterns so that Starr couldn't get the quick pass off to Max. This forced Bart to hesitate throwing the pass, giving the line time to tackle him for the loss.

After the game I remember reporters asking Lombardi why the screen pass hadn't been utilized to slow down the pass rush. Coach responded with, "Starr can't work the screen. He can do a great many things, but that's not one of them."

Detroit's right tackle Roger Brown was all over Starr. He was a 303-pound lineman with blazing speed. During training camp, Brown had raced former track star Glenn Davis in a 25-yard dash. Davis had won gold medals in the longer dashes in both the 1956 and 1960 Olympics, but Roger outran him by a step at 25 yards and barely lost at 50 yards.

Bart later told reporters that he had never been rushed like that in his life.

While the Detroit defense justifiably received the credit for opening up the game, it actually was the two impressive passes from Plum to end Gail Cogdill that gave Detroit the lead—a lead they would keep until the sound of the final gun.

In the first quarter, with third-and-four to go on the Packers' 33-yard line, we expected Plum to throw a short pass, but he crossed us up. Gail

Cogdill sped down the left sideline with Adderley right on his heels to prevent the short pass. Cogdill somehow got behind Adderley and, with burning speed, raced downfield and made a fingertip catch in the end zone for the score.

The two combined once again in the second quarter when Plum lofted the ball right where Cogdill could catch it—near the back of the end zone.

With the Lions leading 14–0, we fumbled the kickoff and found ourselves deep in our own territory. On third-and-long, Starr searched frantically for a free receiver but was hit by Roger Brown. The hit was so vicious that it caused Bart to fumble the ball. It was recovered on the 6 by Lions defensive end Sam Williams, who brought it in for six, giving Detroit a three-touchdown lead. On the next set, Starr was once again hit by Brown, but this time Roger caught Bart in the Packers end zone for a safety. The score became 23–0.

Just before the first half ended, we began to show some signs of life as we drove to the Lions' 26-yard line. But on fourth down, Jerry Kramer (who was replacing the injured Paul Hornung) attempted a field goal. The kick went wide as the gun sounded, ending the half.

Not only did Detroit sack Starr eight times, but they had limited me to only three yards on eight first-half carries.

Early in the second half Detroit's "Night Train" Lane intercepted a Starr pass on the Lions' 42. Next Plum kicked a 47-yard field goal, giving them a 26–0 lead. Finally, the Pack began to rally.

With the ball on the Lions' 28, Plum was intercepted by our defensive end Bill Quinlan. Startled by the catch, Quinlan ended up fumbling the ball. Luckily for us, our end Willie Davis recovered the ball in the end zone for the touchdown. The play may not have affected the outcome of the game, but it sure irritated Detroit's assistant coach, Scooter McLean. He desperately wanted to shut out the Packers just so he could say that Green Bay couldn't score a touchdown on the Lions all year.

With six minutes left to play in the game, we had one last chance to score. Lions fullback Ken Webb (who replaced the injured Nick Pietrosante) fumbled the ball on his own 14. Once again Willie Davis recovered the ball, and a few plays later I scored from the 4-yard line. Final score: Detroit 26, Packers 14.

The Lions' victory had put them only one game behind us in the Western Division standings. If they had held on to the lead in that first game, they would have been tied with us.

At the end of the game, Lombardi gathered his players around him and told us that the true challenge was now ahead of us. He said, "Let it be an example to all of us. The Green Bay Packers are no better than anyone else when they aren't ready, when they play as individuals and not as one…. Our greatest glory is not in never falling, but in rising every time we fall."

The following week we played the Los Angeles Rams at home and ran all over them, beating them 41–10. Paul was finally back in the lineup and scored on a 30-yard pass from Starr in the first quarter. Kramer was still kicking for Hornung and made the extra point. A short while later, Jerry kicked a 35-yard field goal.

In the second quarter I scored on a one-yard run, and Ron Kramer scored on a four-yard pass. In the third quarter, Jerry once again kicked a field goal—but this time for 37 yards. In the fourth quarter both Earl Gros and I rushed for TDs. I ended up with 16 carries for 71 yards.

Although we had won our game, so did Detroit. We were clinging to a one-game lead over the Lions.

That following Sunday, our one-game lead was beginning to vanish. We were playing San Francisco at Kezar Stadium. At the half the score read 21–10, 49ers. On our way back to the locker room we saw on the scoreboard that the Lions had beaten Minnesota 37–23.

At the beginning of the second half, Bart finally began to connect with his receivers. He hit me with a beautiful pass, and I ran for a first down. He next completed a second pass and then threw a third pass again to me. On that same drive, he handed off to Tom Moore who drove in for the score. But we were still behind 21–17.

San Francisco was unable to move the ball, and we took over with a vengeance. Bart played flawlessly and mixed up his plays just enough to confuse the 49ers defense. He handed off to Hornung, which was good for a first down. Paul then ran through the left tackle for another first down. Bart continued his charismatic play by throwing to Tom Moore, Paul, and then to me for another touchdown. We had pulled ahead of San Francisco,

24–21. We scored another TD before the final gun sounded, and we had a 31–21 victory. We were now certain of at least a tie for the Western Conference title.

We played the Rams in Los Angeles during the final week of the regular season. We left with a narrow 20–17 victory and won our third straight Western Conference championship.

The next stop was New York and a repeat of the previous year's championship game—but this time the Giants were out for vengeance.

Chapter

The 1962 Championship Game: Green Bay at New York, December 30, 1962

A year after the Packers' rout of the Giants in Green Bay, our two teams met again in Yankee Stadium to decide who would go into the New Year as NFL champions. Some 65,000 Giants fans, screaming for revenge, turned out for the game.

The weather was even worse than the previous year, with temperatures during the game dropping from 20 degrees to 10 degrees with high swirling winds of 20 to 30 mph that shut down Y.A. Tittle's attempts at long passes. The roughest conditions for a title game since 1945 pretty much shut down the Packers' passing game as well. The game turned into a low-scoring wrestling match essentially played out at ground level, and at the end of the day the Packers had their record-setting eighth NFL championship.

While in the locker room before the game, Hornung sat in his cubicle smoking a Marlboro. Everyone could tell that he was concerned about his sore shoulder and bruised knee. He could do everything but kick. Jim Ringo was worried about his right arm. It had continued to go numb on him due to a nerve problem. It was hard for him to snap the ball, but he knew Lombardi was counting on him. I wasn't feeling good. I had dropped 15 pounds in only a few weeks. It wouldn't be until a week or so later that the doctors would discover that I was suffering from hepatitis.

After Don Chandler's punt to end the Giants' opening possession resulted in a touchback, the Packers drove the ball downfield. After going 61 yards in 10 plays, the Giants contained me near the goal line, and the result was just a 26-yard Jerry Kramer field goal. (There were 10 Packers on the field for the kick.) The Giants responded with a long drive starting at their 38 and featuring a 21-yard Tittle pass to Del Shofner. From the Packers' 16, Tittle aimed the ball for Joe Walton at the goal line, but Ray Nitschke saved the day by tipping the pass; the ball fell into the hands of Dan Currie at the 10, and Currie took it out to the Packers' 40. We began another strong drive, but this time it ended with Kramer missing a 37-yard field-goal try just as the first quarter ended. On the next kickoff, Johnny Counts took the ball at the 9 and was running upfield for a potential touchdown when Willie Wood tackled him at the Giants' 41. The Giants went three-and-out, and wound up punting.

The big play of the second quarter came from Nitschke. He again recovered a fumble by Phil King at the Giants' 28. From there, Hornung took the handoff and stayed in the backfield to deliver a 21-yard strike to Boyd Dowler. I took the ball in from the 7, and we had a 10–0 lead. Both teams failed to do much else that quarter, and Chandler missed a 47-yard field-goal attempt just before the half.

Midway through the third quarter, we were backed up near our goal line and our punter, Max McGee, took the snap. Erich Barnes came in and blocked McGee's punt, and Giant Jim Collier fell on the ball in the end zone for the touchdown. That narrowed our lead to three. A few minutes later, we punted, and Sam Horner failed to make a shoestring catch. Nitschke was there to fall on the ball at the Giants' 42. The Packers proceeded to convert on a Kramer field goal nine plays later. On our next possession, the Giants took the ball downfield, and Wood was called for pass interference deep in Packers territory. He jumped up to protest the call to back judge

Tom Kelleher, knocking Kelleher down in the process. The personal foul tossed Wood from the game, and it combined with the pass interference to set up the Giants at the Packers' 18. But two holding penalties took the Giants back to the 40, and they wound up not even trying for a field goal, which ended the drive.

With 6:28 left in the fourth quarter, the Giants had a fourth-and-three from their 44 and punted: it was their last real chance at victory. The Packers went back on the march and picked up the clinching Kramer field goal with 1:50 left. Next, we went into a prevent defense and let Tittle drive the Giants down to the Packers' 10 with a 25-yard pass to Joe Walton, and that was the play ended the game. Final score: Packers 16, Giants 7.

Due to the ferocious winds and freezing temperatures, Lombardi had decided to discard his aerial attack and put the offensive game in the hands of Hornung and me. I gained a total of 85 yards running and carried the ball 31 times. At the end of each run I was smacked down on the frozen tundra. But it was the Giants' middle linebacker Sam Huff who was the most aggressive when it came to hitting me or piling on.

When everyone finally climbed off the pile, I would get up and just look at Sam, spit, and say, "Is that your best shot?"

It would drive Sam crazy.

Nitschke took away MVP honors for his part in the three Giants turnovers, and we used our general strength and ruggedness to shut down the Giants and muster enough offense for the win.

After the game, Coach Lombardi described the game to the press by saying, "Gentlemen, you have just seen a truly great football game. In my opinion, this was as fine a football game as has ever been played. There was great tackling, great blocking, great running, and great pursuit on the part of both teams. My boys were superb on defense."

Bart was next in line to talk to the media, and he said, "The wind really was fierce, but you had to live with it. In all my years of football, that was the trickiest wind I've ever seen. You couldn't tell which direction it was coming from or where it was going to.

"This win was even a bigger thrill than last year. We were playing in Yankee Stadium before a hostile crowd, and we knew that if we wanted to have any pride over the winter, we had to win this game."

Then Kramer spoke about his field goals: "I just aimed for the middle [of the goalposts] and prayed. It's the first game [where] my kicking ever made the difference on the scoreboard—and boy, it felt great."

I told the press, "I never took a worse beating on a football field. The Giants hit me hard, and then I hit the ground hard. I got it both ways. This was the toughest game I've ever played. I had stitches taken in my elbow at halftime, but that wasn't the half of it. I bit my tongue in the first quarter when Sam Huff tackled me, and [I] was spitting up blood the whole game, but I just rammed it down their throats by letting my running do my talking. They couldn't rattle me."

In my opinion, our 1962 Packers team was the best. We not only averaged 30 points per game, but also we basically scored at will. Our defense was incredible. To let you know how good a team we really were, 11 of our players were voted to the All-Pro team—and that's when there were only 22 players total on the team!

On offense we had Ron and Jerry Kramer, Forrest Gregg, Fuzzy Thurston, Jim Ringo, and me. On defense, it was Willie Davis, Henry Jordan, Dan Currie, Bill Forester, and Herb Adderley.

Ironically Starr didn't make the All-Pro team even after leading the league in passing, and Willie Wood didn't make it even though he led the league in interceptions!

For me, it was a great year. I ended up leading the league in rushing with a total of 1,474 yards compared to Cleveland's Jim Brown, who rushed for a total of 996 yards. That single-season yardage mark of 1,474 was not surpassed by a Packer until Ahman Green ran for 1,883 yards in 2003.

Chapter

Scandal in the NFL

On April 17, 1963, the world of professional football awoke to the shocking headlines in their morning papers: "Hornung and Karras Suspended Indefinitely."

To some of the guys, the news had not been unexpected. Throughout the 1962 season, there were rumors floating around that commissioner Pete Rozelle had contacted the FBI and asked them to check on alleged gambling among the players. There is an NFL rule that strictly prohibits betting on games among its players. The big question: were games being thrown?

Not long after we had returned to Green Bay after winning the championship, FBI investigators contacted Max McGee and requested that he report to their Chicago office for questioning.

When McGee met with the feds, he found out that it wasn't him that they were interested in—it was Paul Hornung. They wanted to question McGee because he had been Paul's roommate. They had been taping Paul's conversations for quite a while.

Later Paul's other roommate, Ron Kramer, was questioned by investigators in Detroit. He had little, if anything at all, to say.

When Detroit played Green Bay during the regular season, some of the Detroit players—Joe Schmidt, Wayne Walker, John Gordy, Sam Williams, and Gary Lowe—had bet $50 each on a Green Bay win. They had never placed a bet on the outcome of a league game before, but the rule had been broken, and each were given a $2,000 fine. The Lions ballclub was given a $2,000 fine for ignoring reports of gambling by its players.

In the end it was Hornung and Detroit's Alex Karras who would be slapped with breaking the NFL rule. Even though they both said that their bets were social, Rozelle was not amused.

The only course of action was to suspend both Paul and Alex indefinitely.

Although the suspension of two of the league's top players was intense, Rozelle seemed somewhat relieved and said to the press, "There is no evidence that any NFL player has given less than his best in playing any game. There is no evidence that any player has ever bet against his own team. There is no evidence that any NFL player has sold information to gamblers. There is clear evidence that some NFL players knowingly carried on undesirable associations, which, in some instances, led to their betting on their own team to win and/or other National Football League games."

Everyone knew how much Lombardi wanted to be the first team to win three titles in a row, and the press predicted that Starr would lead us to a fourth consecutive Western Conference crown and an undisputed third-straight NFL championship despite the loss of Paul.

No one considered the incredible strength and talent of the Chicago Bears or the injuries that would plague the Packers throughout the 1963 season.

Chapter

The College All-Star Game

The first game of the year was the annual All-Star game at Soldier Field in Chicago between the NFL champions and the College All-Stars. The game was always a total mismatch—what one sportswriter called "A contest of men against boys." Hell, the last time the All-Stars won a game against the NFL champs was back in 1958 against the Detroit Lions. But no one could predict the outcome of this game.

The All-Stars lineup included Dave Robinson, a two-way end from Penn State, and defensive tackle Bobby Bell from Minnesota. Anchoring the offensive line was Michigan State guard Ed Budde. The quarterback, Ron VanderKelen, was out of Wisconsin, as was his catching partner, end Pat Richter.

The game was played in humid conditions, and the majority of the Packers were not yet in playing shape. No one really seemed too worried about the game—that is, until it was too late.

VanderKelen hit Richter for a touchdown late in the game, giving the All-Stars a 10-point lead, which they held on to—winning the game 20–17.

Lombardi was visibly embarrassed by the loss and proved it by making practice that week a living hell. All-Stars Dave Robinson and Tony Liscio— both of whom were drafted by Green Bay—tell of the treatment they received by Lombardi the Monday following the loss. It is a day that Robinson will never forget. "I arrived 15 minutes ahead of schedule for my first team meeting a few days after the game. When I entered the room, Lombardi was already there. He didn't say a word to me. We were getting ready to review film of the All-Star game. I thought it would be good because I had had a good game—especially against Ron Kramer.

"When it came to that play, Lombardi stopped the projector. I thought that he was going to compliment me. Instead, he yelled at Ron Kramer by telling him, 'Look at that rookie get rid of you. That kid probably won't even make the team that drafted him!'

"I slouched into my seat. Lombardi didn't even know who I was!"

Liscio received a similar reception. He said, "It was tough going back to the hotel where the Packers were staying after the All-Star Game to have dinner with them. You could hear a pin drop.

"Lombardi made us have a full scrimmage that following Monday. Monday was usually a light practice day. Vince was raving mad. It became a sweet and sour victory for me. I was originally an offensive tackle, but Lombardi put me on defense. After five weeks, he traded me to the Dallas Cowboys, where they switched me back to offensive tackle and I got to start my first year. Lombardi said later that he had made a mistake by trading me."

Chapter 26

A Three-Peat?

The idea of winning three championships in a row consumed Lombardi.

The first game of the year wasagainst the Chicago Bears. George Halas had just signed a new defensive coordinator, George Allen. Allen studied Green Bay's offense and found a way to eventually thwart our offensive tendencies.

We ended up losing the game 10–3, and Lombardi was beside himself after the game. To make matters worse, he decided to quit smoking, cold turkey. Lombardi gained 20 pounds but never smoked another cigarette again.

The Packers made up for their losses to the All-Stars and to the Bears by winning eight games in a row against Detroit, Baltimore (twice), Los Angeles, Minnesota (twice), St. Louis, and Pittsburgh. With five games left in the regular season, we really thought we had a good chance to three-peat, but there were two factors that could quite possibly prevent us from being world champions once again.

First of all the Chicago Bears were keeping pace with Green Bay and were tied with us for the league lead. Second of all, and worse, was the injury to Bart Starr. While playing St. Louis, Bart was viciously tackled by one of the Cardinals players, causing him to break his hand. He would not see action for a month.

Lombardi acquired Zeke Bratkowski from the Rams to help John Roach take over for Starr, but the efforts were fruitless as we lost a crucial game to the Bears 26–7.

The loss had really hurt Lombardi, but it was nothing compared to the news that was to come.

On Friday, November 22, 1963—two days before our game against San Francisco—Coach received the news that President John Kennedy had been assassinated in Dallas. He and Kennedy had become good friends throughout the years, and his death had a great affect on him.

We had just finished up practice when the team got word about the president. We were all in the parking lot gathered around our car radios. Lombardi left for church to pray for the fallen president.

That weekend most athletic events were canceled, but the NFL continued game play. Pete Rozelle issued a statement defending his decision to continue: "It has been traditional in sports for athletes to perform in times of great personal tragedy. Football was Mr. Kennedy's game. He thrived on competition."

Chapter

Lost Dreams of a Championship

With only four regular-season games remaining and Chicago leading the Western Conference, Bart Starr returned to the Packers in time to play San Francisco. He was as effective as ever as we rolled over the 49ers 28–10. That same day, the Bears tied the Steelers, which dropped them to a half-game lead over the Pack.

Thanksgiving Day tradition had us competing once again against the Detroit Lions. We watched Bart return to action, only to lose Ray Nitschke to a broken arm. Final score: Packers 13, Lions 13. A tie!

The final two games were away—at Los Angeles and San Francisco. During the 49ers game, I achieved my fourth consecutive 1,000-yard season. The honor was sweet, but the season had a bitter ending.

We had won both of our last two games, but so did Chicago. Even though they had tied twice, the Bears finished the regular season in first place—half a game ahead of us. The final records had Chicago at 11–1–2 and Green Bay at 11–2–1. Chicago had won the conference.

We ended up playing in what was called the Playoff Bowl, which was a game for the runners-up held in Miami. We beat the Browns 40–23 in the Playoff Bowl, but the win didn't make us feel any better about coming in second.

Chapter

The Magic Was Slipping Away

The 1964 season started off well with the reinstatement of Hornung in March. But no sooner did Lombardi welcome back his star halfback than he sent Jim Ringo and Earl Gros to the Eagles for linebacker Lee Roy Caffey and a first-round draft choice.

Ringo's departure from the Packers was quite different from previous trades.

That spring, Jim had met with Lombardi in his office to negotiate his 1964 contract. But this time he brought along something else—a new negotiating tool called an agent. Even though Ringo had been All-Pro, was captain of the offense, and had not missed a game in 10 seasons, Lombardi was insulted by the presence of his agent. Lombardi felt that an agent interfered with the one-on-one personal relationship he had with each of his players.

Coach excused himself from the meeting and returned a few minutes later only to let Jim's agent know that he had been traded to the Eagles.

It was a season of revenge in 1964, and what better way to begin the payback than with a humiliating 23–12 win over our nemesis and reigning world champs, the Chicago Bears. But revenge would be short-lived.

Jerry Kramer had become seriously ill with stomach problems and ended up not suiting up for the remainder of the year. At first it was thought that Kramer had stomach cancer, but tests later proved that his body had become infected by a seven-and-a-half-inch sliver of wood that had lodged in his abdomen during an accident as a teenager and that had gone unde-tected for many years.

Following the opening game of the season, the magic of Hornung's toe lost its accuracy and became undependable. We lost our second game of the year to the Colts by a score of 21–20 and the difference in the game was a missed extra point by Hornung. In the fourth game, Minnesota blocked an extra point to win the game 24–23. In our second game against the Colts, Baltimore beat us 24–21. Paul missed four field-goal attempts and had one blocked.

The remainder of the season saw us beating Detroit, Cleveland, Dallas, and the Bears for a second time. We tied the Rams in our final game of the year. I rushed for more than 1,000 yards for the fifth year in a row, but once again it was a bittersweet season. Our club record was 8–5–1, and we finished second in the Western Division.

We received our invitation to the Playoff Bowl for the second year in a row, but this time we lost 24–17 to the Cardinals. Lombardi referred to the Playoff Bowl as the Shit Bowl. He called it a losers bowl for losers.

Prior to the start of the 1965 season, Bart Starr spoke at his alma mater, the University of Alabama. This is what he told the audience: "Winning is everything. The Packers of 1964 [didn't win], but [we gave] the game [our] best effort. We did all we could. Next year, we may do better."

And we did do better. We made some good trades, and with Coach Lombardi at the helm, we did much better in '65. As a matter of fact, we were the best.

Chapter

Winning Isn't Everything— It's the Only Thing!

During the first day of the 1965 training camp, Lombardi was still visibly upset about his second-place finishes in 1963 and 1964. He delivered the following ultimatum to his team: "This year we are going to be number one! If you don't think we're number one, I don't want you playing for me! If you can't go out there and win, pack your gear and go home!"

Well, no one packed their gear, and no one went home. But it was time for Lombardi to reassess his players for the 1965 season. Hornung had lost most of his kicking abilities due to injuries, and Lombardi needed to find a kicker who could be relied on for game-winning field goals. He found that person in Don Chandler.

Chandler had been a great kicker for the Giants since 1956. Lombardi persuaded him to play for Green Bay and negotiated the trade with New York coach Allie Sherman.

Other important additions to the team included receiver Carroll Dale from the Rams, Georgia Tech center Bill Curry, and a quick running back from the University of Washington by the name of Junior Coffey. Ron Kramer was sent to the Lions.

Our first game was against the Steelers at Pittsburgh. We ran right through them and won the game 41–9. Our second game was against the Colts at home. It was 10–10 in the third quarter when Bart was hit hard by Ordell Braase, the tough Baltimore tight end. Starr's leg was turned under him. He was badly hurt and was unable to get up.

Zeke Bratkowski took his place, and we ended up with our second win, 20–17.

We beat both the Bears and 49ers next, giving us a 4–0 record. On October 17, 1965, we traveled to Detroit to play the Lions.

The clock ticked down, ending the first half in Detroit with the Lions up 21–3. The Packers and Lombardi began to run off the field. Just as we were heading for the tunnel, the Lions' defensive tackle, Alex Karras, yelled out to Lombardi, "Whadaya think of that, ya big, fat wop!"

Karras held a personal hatred for the Packers and loved nothing more than to beat Green Bay. The Lions had won three out of their first four games and would be tied with us if they could have held on to the lead— but that was not to be. The second half was all Green Bay, which seemed to shut up Karras. We won by a score of 31–21.

In the sixth week we took on the Cowboys and easily won the game 13–3. But Week 7 against the Bears proved unfortunate for our undefeated season and our quarterback.

Chicago was out to avenge their two straight defeats at the hands of Green Bay. In the second quarter we were ahead 7–3 when Starr faded back to pass. All of his receivers were covered, so he decided to take it himself. As he ran, twisted, and dodged his way up the field, he ran into Bears defensive back Roosevelt Taylor. Bart went down hard. Lombardi quickly pulled Starr out of the game and replaced him with Bratkowski.

Bart should have stayed out for the remainder of the game, but in a few minutes he was back in calling the signals. He told Lombardi that he was OK, but he wasn't. His timing was off, and he called the wrong plays at the wrong times.

Not only did we end up losing 31–10 to the Bears, but we were now tied with Baltimore for the Western Conference lead.

Bart was still plagued by the injury when we met Detroit on November 7. His form was off, and his passing was erratic. The Lions continued to attack and went on to win 12–7. Our record fell to 6–2.

We played the Rams at home and, lucky for us, Chandler's kicking was accurate. With just 37 seconds left in the game, Chandler booted his 13th field goal of the season to beat the Rams 6–3.

By the time we played the Vikings on November 21, Starr was as good as new. He proved he was ready to play by throwing three touchdown passes as we routed the Vikes 38–13. On the downside, Baltimore kept winning, and Green Bay was still one full game behind the Colts.

With an unexpected loss to the Rams and a decisive win over Minnesota, our record after 12 games was 9–3. The Colts led the conference with a 9–2–1 record while the Bears were only one game behind the Pack with an 8–4 record. Our next game was against the Colts in Baltimore with the title still up for grabs.

On a cold December 12 in Baltimore, the fog was so thick that at times we couldn't see in front of us. But that didn't stop the Pack. From the first quarter until the final gun sounded, Green Bay never looked back. If ever the Colts needed Johnny Unitas, they needed him that day.

The Bears had knocked Unitas out for the season the week before, and the young quarterback who replaced him, Gary Cuozzo, could not compete against the tough veterans of Green Bay. Final score: Packers 42, Colts 27.

With one more regular-season game to go, Baltimore was now a half game behind us. A victory over San Francisco the following week would clinch the title for Green Bay. But if the Packers lost and the Colts won, then the Colts would win the title. The Bears could not be counted out yet either. They were only one game behind us. Chicago needed to win and for Baltimore and us to lose in order to capture the crown. And that's what almost happened.

Baltimore won their game on Sunday, eliminating the Bears from the race, but we weren't as fortunate. In the second quarter, Starr threw for his only passing touchdown of the day, and in the fourth quarter I rushed five yards into the end zone. Later that same quarter, Chandler kicked a 31-yard field goal, giving the Packers a 24–17 lead.

But with only a little less than a minute left in the game, 49ers quarterback John Brodie hit Vern Burke for a 27-yard score (and an extra point by kicker Tommy Davis) to even up the score and end the game in a 24–24 tie.

The race for the Western Conference championship was deadlocked. We were to meet the Colts one last time to decide who would take on the Eastern Conference champions, the Cleveland Browns, for the NFL world championship.

Chapter

The 1965 Playoffs: Baltimore at Green Bay, December 26, 1965

The game against Baltimore was scheduled for December 26, 1965, in Wisconsin. The Colts arrived in Green Bay on December 25. Not only had they lost Johnny Unitas to injuries but also his backup quarterback Gary Cuozzo. Halfback Tom Matte had been converted to the quarterback position.

When the Packers entered their locker room on the day of the game, there was a sign taped above each player's locker. Lombardi had quoted from another of Red Blaik's signature phrases. The sign read, "Anything Is Ours…Providing We Are Willing to Pay the Price!"

With that in mind, we walked out onto the field. The crowd that jammed the Packers stands let out an incredible roar. The two team captains met, the coin was tossed, and Green Bay won and elected to receive. The crowd went wild, but not for long.

The Colts kicked off, and we began our march from our own 15-yard line. Bart faked to me, then threw a short pass to Bill Anderson. Anderson caught the pass but was hit hard by Baltimore cornerback Lenny Lyles. Bill fumbled, and Colts linebacker Don Shinnick began running down the field with only one person to stop him—Starr. Shinnick ran right over Bart and into the Green Bay end zone for a 25-yard return TD.

In the meantime, Bart lay still on the ground. His chest and rib cage were badly bruised. That was his first and last play of the game. He would only be utilized as a place-kick holder. As the gun sounded to end the half, the Colts were on top 10–0.

In the third quarter, Hornung rushed for a one-yard TD and Chandler kicked the PAT. The score was 10–7.

With only two minutes left in the game, Chandler once more came through for the Pack and kicked a field goal that tied the game. The gun sounded once more, but this time to end the game with a 10–10 tie. We would play an extra period, known as sudden death. The conference championship would be decided on which team scored first.

The first 13 minutes saw no score by either team. In the 10th minute of overtime, Colts kicker Lou Michaels attempted a field goal from the Green Bay 47, and it was no good. With less than two minutes remaining in this dramatic battle of dominance, Chandler and Starr stepped on to the field.

The ball was on the Baltimore 25-yard line. Bart took the snap from center and placed the ball precisely where Chandler could kick it. As the ball sailed directly between the goalposts, a deafening roar came from the crowd. Final score: Green Bay 13, Baltimore 10.

The *Green Bay Gazette* called it one of the most dramatic games in NFL history.

Chapter 31

The 1965 Championship Game: Cleveland at Green Bay, January 2, 1966

The NFL Championship Game between the Packers and the Cleveland Browns was played in Green Bay on January 2, 1966. That day three inches of snow fell on Lambeau Field. The snow later turned to rain and the rain to sleet. But that didn't stop the 50,853 screaming fans from attending the match.

That day, Starr was still hurting, but he started for the Packers and led our team as it took the opening kickoff and went 77 yards in seven plays for the first seven points. Starr's 47-yard pass to Carroll Dale scored the touchdown. Walter Beach bit on a fake by Dale and fell down at the 20 as Dale got the pass, leaving him with plenty of room to run into the end zone. Immediately afterward, though, Charles Scales ran back the kickoff 14 yards to start the Browns off at their 34. Jim Brown outwrestled David Robinson for the ball and hauled in a 30-yard pass from Frank Ryan. Ryan followed it up with a 19-yard throw to Paul Warfield. The Browns were at the 17, and Ryan kept passing, this time to Gary Collins, open in the end zone for the touchdown. Bob Franklin flubbed the snap for the PAT, and Lou Groza was left to pick up the ball and throw it to Franklin, who was tackled by Willie Wood shy of the goal line. There were 13 points scored in the first five minutes of the game.

Soon after, the Browns took advantage of a 31-yard punt that put them at the Packers' 39, capping a short drive with a 24-yard Groza field goal. At the 17, Ryan had overthrown Warfield in the end zone. Our offense responded on its next drive, going 73 yards. The highlight was a 34-yard run by Hornung to the Browns' 3. But when Starr took a five-yard sack, we settled for a 15-yard field goal by Don Chandler early in the second quarter.

Just a few minutes later, Wood caught an interception and ran it 15 yards to the Browns' 15. Starr threw three straight incompletions, and we had to settle for a field goal. It was countered by a 28-yard Groza field goal just before the half. At that point, the Packers had 158 yards to 135 for the Browns and 34 plays to Cleveland's 23.

In the second half, we held Brown to nine yards, and the Browns had only 26 yards—15 on the ground and 11 by air. The Browns had just 16 plays in the closing two quarters—11 in the third and five in the fourth— leaving the Packers free to control the ball with 35 plays. For the entire game, we had 69 plays to the Browns' 39. The half featured a 90-yard, 11-play Packers drive in the third quarter that lasted seven minutes and ended with a power sweep by Hornung that used Forrest Gregg and Kramer for a 13-yard touchdown run. The Browns then had their only real drive of the half, getting the ball to the Packers' 27. But when Groza came on for a 37-yard field goal, it was partially blocked by Henry Jordan, and the ball came to a stop in the end zone for a touchback.

After the block, we held the ball for a drive that lasted nearly eight minutes and ended with Chandler's last field goal, which tied him for the NFL title game record of three. Later on, a roughing-the-punter call on Browns end Ralph Smith rescued Chandler from having to punt from his own end zone, and by the game's final two minutes, Lombardi was confident enough of victory to pull out his starters one by one, leaving Starr for last. The Packers had their ninth NFL title, one more than the eight tallied by the Bears. The capacity crowd of 50,852 hollered and cheered, and many flooded the field to mingle with us and tear down the goalposts.

The game was played on a slippery field in snow, sleet, rain, and fog, with temperatures in the low 30s. After the game, Jim Brown said, "The mud restricted movement. There were certain moves I couldn't make that I normally make. I was running into people that I normally would get by."

Brown's longest run in the game was for 14 yards. The Browns were missing tackle Dick Schafrath with an injury. But of course, great play by our defensive line had something to do with Brown's showing too, and in turn, the Green Bay linemen did a lot to get Hornung and me 201 combined rushing yards.

In the locker room, Hornung said to the press, "Taylor and I are just a couple of old-timers trying to hang on. It was a very satisfying game for me—particularly when four or five weeks ago everybody said I was through."

At the end of the game I was named the game's MVP. Cooper Hollow of the *Chicago Tribune* wrote an article titled "Happy Packers Had Many Heroes—Taylor Is MVP of Game." In it, he penned:

> His face was as grimy as the inside of a blast furnace. His uniform was so muddy that the number 31 on the back of his jersey was indistinguishable.
>
> Jim Taylor, still holding his helmet, stood erect in the center of the dressing room surrounded by dozens of newsmen.
>
> How'd you do it, Jimmy? Did the slippery field bother you? How bad did the leg hurt?
>
> These were among the questions hurled late today at the Green Bay Packers fullback, who minutes before had put the finishing touches to a 23–12 victory over the Cleveland Browns and the elements for the National Football League title.

Teammates Answer

Fuzzy Thurston and Jerry Kramer didn't give Taylor a chance to answer. The two Packer guards, both heroes in their own right on this happy January Sabbath, busted through the cluster of reports and threw their arms around Taylor.

"Didn't I tell you, Jimmy; didn't I tell you?" shouted Kramer. "I told you you'd have a great afternoon."

Taylor, by gaining 96 yards in 27 crashing runs through the Cleveland line, won a sports car as the game's Most Valuable Player.

Has His Number

Jimmy gets to keep his # 31, said Thurston. Grabowski will have to look for a different number. (Jim Grabowski, Illinois fullback recently signed by the Packers, also wears #31).

Taylor just smiled—a big ol' cigar clenched between his teeth. Green Bay was once again Titletown USA.

Chapter

The Winds of Change

The year 1966 brought incredible changes to the NFL and to the structure of the gridiron world. After a series of meetings between the National Football League and the American Football League, an amalgamation of great stature was about to take place.

On June 8, 1966, commissioner Pete Rozelle made an announcement that stunned the world of professional football. He said, "It has been decided that in 1970 both the National Football League and the American Football League will merge and become the National Football League. The teams will be divided between the National Football Conference [the NFC] and the American Football Conference [the AFC].

"At the end of the 1966 season, the champions of the NFL will meet the champions of the AFL for the championship of the world in what will be called the Super Bowl."

Lombardi was elated with the idea of a new Super Bowl championship, but at the same time was fully aware that Hornung's and my playing days were numbered. He also knew that he would have to dig deep to find adequate replacements for both Paul and me.

In 1966 it was also the year of the six-figure contract and the sports agent. Lombardi wasn't keen on either of them, but he knew in order to complete, he would have to change with the times.

Two running backs were eventually acquired by Green Bay—Jim Grabowski, a star back out of the University of Illinois, and Donny Anderson, an All-American out of Texas Tech. But the means of how they would be acquired would not be an easy one for Lombardi to swallow.

Grabowski brought in his attorney, and they settled on a three-year contract in the amount of $400,000. Anderson also signed with Green Bay but was offered a $500,000 package. After finding out how much the two untested rookies would be making, I decided that I would play for the Packers one more year and finish out my contact, but I kept it to myself.

Chapter

My Final Year in the Green and Gold

Our Packers team went right after the Western Conference championship from the opening game of the season. We ran all over the Colts 24–3. Our second game was against the Browns in Cleveland. They were eager for revenge after their defeat to us in the 1965 title game, and they almost got even.

We were on our own 19-yard line with 2:34 remaining in the game. Cleveland was leading 20–14. Starr began to march his troops down the field—a pass to Boyd Dowler, another pass to Marv Fleming, and a pass to Donny Anderson. It was third down, and the clock was ticking away.

Bart called a quarterback sneak and charged through the line for the first down. With only seconds to go, Starr took the snap from center, faked a pass, then spotted me in the end zone. With a short swing pass that fell right on the numbers, I scored. Chandler booted the extra point, and we beat the Browns 21–20. We had moved the ball 85 yards in 14 plays.

We beat the Rams and Lions at home to give us a 4–0 record, then traveled to San Francisco to play the 49ers.

The 49ers had lost all of their preseason games, tied the Vikings in the home opener, and lost to Baltimore and Los Angles before playing us. They ended up beating us 21–20.

On October 16, we shut out the Bears in Chicago by a score of 17–0, and on October 23, we annihilated the Falcons 56–3 at home. After that game, Ken Hartnett, a sports reporter for the Associated Press in Milwaukee, came over to my locker for an interview.

I was visibly upset that Lombardi didn't put me in the game more, and Hartnett knew it. He asked me about a rumor that had been going around. He asked, "Are you going to play out your option with the Packers?"

"Yeah," I said, and added that the large salaries paid to Anderson and Grabowski had been an insult to my pride.

Hartnett wrote the story, and when Lombardi read it in Monday's paper, he erupted. He ordered Tom Miller, one of his publicists, to find me and bring me in for an explanation.

When I reached Lombardi's office, he held up a copy of the paper and screamed, "Explain this!"

I claimed that I had been misquoted.

Lombardi then announced that he was banning Hartnett from all pregame and postgame press conferences and also from the Packers' locker room.

Later that day, a petition was drafted to Commissioner Rozelle by the Wisconsin sportswriters protesting the coach's action. Because of an NFL policy that would not allow accredited writers to be banned from press boxes, clubhouses, or dressing rooms, Lombardi was forced to withdraw his complaint.

Lombardi knew that Hartnett's story was accurate. He knew that I would not sign his contract and was privately waiting to leave at the end of the 1966 season. The fact that this information went public infuriated Lombardi. The fact that the people were made aware that I wanted out of Green Bay challenged Lombardi's total control.

It was about this time that Coach began getting dizzy spells and blackouts. His drive to win had begun to consume him both physically and mentally.

We continued our winning streak by beating the Lions 31–7 in Detroit, only to have our second and last loss of the season come 20–17 at home to Minnesota.

We finished the regular season by beating the Bears at home, the Vikings in Minnesota, the 49ers at home, and the Colts and Rams away. Our record was 12–2–0, and it was our fifth Western Conference championship in seven years.

Chapter 34

The 1966 Championship Game: Green Bay at Dallas, January 1, 1967

The National Football League title game would be played on January 1, 1967, against the Dallas Cowboys and coach Tom Landry. Even though Lombardi and Landry were both assistants for Jim Lee Howell in New York, they had always competed against each other. This time would be no different.

The Cowboys in 1966 became the first expansion team to win a conference title and were now prepared to meet us in what turned out to be one of the most exciting NFL title games. A packed Cotton Bowl crowd of 74,152 fans was kept on the edge of their seats as both teams fought it out for the next four hours.

In the first quarter, Elijah Pitts busted through a big hole in the Dallas defense and ran 34 yards on the first play of the game. A few plays later, Starr threw a 17-yard touchdown to Pitts for the first score of the game.

Within the next 12 seconds we had doubled our lead. Dallas free safety Mel Renfro fumbled the kickoff, and our rookie Jim Grabowski scooped up the ball and ran it 18 yards into the end zone for a second score.

The Cowboys came back with two quick drives as running backs Dan Reeves, who rushed for three yards, and Don Perkins, who rushed for 23 yards, found their way through our defense for the scores.

In the second quarter Starr hit Carroll Dale on a 51-yard bomb for a score, but Cowboys kicker Danny Villanueva kicked two field goals—one from the 11-yard line in the second quarter and another from the 32 in the third. It became a one-point game with us ahead 21–20.

Starr found both Dowler and McGee and we went up 34–20 early in the fourth quarter.

Don Meredith then hit Frank Clarke on a 68-yard touchdown play to cut our lead to 34–27.

With only 30 seconds left in the game, it came down to one play. On fourth down, the Cowboys were on our 2-yard line and threatening to score. Meredith called a rollout to the right, but our left linebacker, Dave Robinson, broke through and forced Meredith to throw uncontrollably. Instead of it landing in the hands of Cowboy Bob Hayes—the fastest man on the field—it landed in the hands of our free safety, Tom Brown, and ended the game.

Once again, Green Bay had won the title. Next up was the world championship, or what was now called the Super Bowl.

Super Bowl I: Green Bay vs. Kansas City, January 15, 1967

The day before the championship game we were all at our hotel in Los Angeles. That afternoon Max McGee met a couple of stewardesses at the hotel bar and agreed to meet them later that night. He told Paul Hornung his situation, but Paul declined the offer. His shoulder was still bothering him, and the thought of having to pay thousands of dollars in fines for breaking curfew did not interest him.

Hawg Hanner, a retired former Packer, was our assistant coach. He was in charge of curfew bed checks. The evening before the game, he stuck his head into Max and Paul's room to be sure they were in bed. Minutes after Hanner had left the room, so did McGee.

Max returned the following morning just in time to see Bart Starr walking through the lobby. When McGee returned to his room, he asked

Paul if he was safe. Paul told him no. Max didn't take it to heart and decided to take an hour nap before boarding the bus for the game.

There was no fanfare or worldwide creative advertising as there is today. The words *Super Bowl* didn't even have the Roman numeral *I* after them; it was just Super Bowl.

The game would be watched by the largest television audience ever to view a sports event—more than 65 million people—but inside the Memorial Coliseum it felt almost empty. The Coliseum holds 100,000 people. Only 61,946 showed up for the championship game. The most expensive ticket cost $12, yet the stadium was only two-thirds full. Pete Rozelle gave Ed Sabol (who at that time was the president of NFL Films) 15 complimentary tickets. Ed, in turn, gave them to his cameramen to give out. They came back with five Super Bowl tickets that they couldn't even give away!

Once the game had begun, Hornung and McGee sat next to each other on the bench. All of a sudden they heard the deafening sound of Lombardi's voice: "McGeeeeeeeee!"

Max's initial thought was that it was over for him and that Lombardi would release him right then and there on the field. But that was not the case. He had yelled for Max to get in the game. Boyd Dowler had tried to play, but his shoulder was still in too much pain from the Dallas game. All of a sudden, McGee had his eye on the '67 silver Corvette convertible that *Sport* magazine was giving to the MVP of the game. In the next series, Max caught a Starr pass for a 37-yard touchdown. He ended the day with seven catches and two touchdowns for a total of 138 yards, but it would be Starr who would win the MVP honors and drive away in the new silver Corvette.

Early in the second quarter both teams were tied at 7, but that would soon change. On third-and-five from our own 32, Starr passed to McGee for 10 yards, then to Dale for 15, then to Marv Fleming for 11. He found Pitts in the flat and picked up 10 more, putting the ball on Kansas City's 14. From there I went to Starr's left, cut back behind blocks by Jerry Kramer and Fuzzy Thurston, and covered the 14 yards to put us ahead 14–7. That score also made me the first NFL player to score a rushing touchdown in a Super Bowl. From that point on, we were never behind again.

During the game there was an incident between Kansas City defensive tackle Buck Buchanan and me. We exchanged a few words after Buchanan hit me with a forearm. I'd been thrown down before by bigger and stronger men. The play was over, the whistle had blown, and still he had to be a hero. I just turned my back and walked away from him.

Once Lombardi knew that the game was ours, he sent in Zeke Bratkowski along with most of our second stringers to give them the opportunity to play in the championship game.

The gun sounded to an anticlimactic game finish—Packers 35, Kansas City 10—but it gave the Packers the undisputed title to the world football crown.

Following the game, McGee officially retired. In the locker room he told the press, "Sayonara. It's a great game to quit on, and I quit!"

The 1967 Super Bowl was the last time I suited up in a Green Bay Packers uniform.

Chapter

Characters, Heroes, and Great Leading Men

Ten of Lombardi's boys made it to the Pro Football Hall of Fame as Packers. With the exception of Paul Hornung, the rest of us were either underrated by the pro scouts or completely unnoticed. But the things we all had in common were the desire to win and to play beyond our abilities, and our loyalty to our team and coach.

Packers in the Hall of Fame
Herb Adderley (1961–1969)
Cornerback 6'0", 205 lbs. (Michigan State)
1961–1969 Green Bay Packers, 1970–1972 Dallas Cowboys
HOF Class of 1980
When Herb reported to his first Green Bay training camp in 1961 as the Packers' No.1 draft pick, he first had to compete against Paul Hornung and me for a starter's spot. That was the first and only time I ever saw Paul worried about losing his starting job. Adderley had played running back

for Michigan State, and that's the position where Lombardi played him for the first few days of practice. He was big and he was fast. Midway through the season, however, Lombardi utilized Herb as an emergency replacement for our injured starting cornerback, Hank Gremminger. It turned out to be the decision that paved the way for him to make the Hall of Fame.

Herb was the first to define the corner position as we still know it today. Adderley had great athleticism, and he was in such good shape that I don't ever remember seeing him breathing hard. He could run backward faster than most guys could run forward, and he aggressively went after the football.

He showed Lombardi that he had what it took to be an NFL cornerback. He won All-NFL honors in 1962, 1963, 1965, and 1966. Lombardi once admitted that he almost made a mistake with Adderley. He said, "I was too stubborn to switch him to defense until I had to. Now when I think of what Adderley means to our defense, it scares me to think of how I almost mishandled him."

Between 1961 and 1969 Herb intercepted 39 passes. He also doubled as a kickoff-return specialist during the majority of his career with the Packers and wound up with a 25.7-yard average on 120 returns. Two of those returns included a 103-yard return in 1962 and a 98-yard run in 1963. He played in five Pro Bowl games during the 1960s.

Adderley played in four of the first six Super Bowl games, winning three championship rings. He also played in seven NFL Championship Games in an 11-year span from 1961 through 1971. In the 33–14 Packers win over Oakland in Super Bowl II, he returned an interception 60 yards for a touchdown, which was the only interception return for a touchdown in the first 10 Super Bowls.

After being traded from Green Bay following the 1969 season, he played three years for the Dallas Cowboys.

Willie Davis (1960–1969)
Defensive End 6'3", 243 lbs. (Grambling)
1958–1959 Cleveland Browns, 1960–1969 Green Bay Packers
HOF Class of 1981

To say that Willie Davis' pro football career got off to a bad start would be an understatement. First the Cleveland Browns drafted him in 1956, but the army took precedence over the NFL, and he didn't join the team until 1958. In his first two seasons, he played only briefly at several different positions. By the time he was ready for a regular offensive-tackle job in 1960, he was traded to the Packers.

Willie, surprised and upset by this sudden move, considered quitting, but Lombardi assured him that the Packers needed a good defensive end and that he was the guy for the job. Lombardi told him, "I consider speed, agility, and size to be the three most important attributes in a successful lineman. Give me a man who has any two of those dimensions, and he'll do okay. But give him all three, and he'll be great. We think you have all three."

Davis also had dedication, intelligence, and leadership ability, which enabled him to rise a cut above the others. In his 12-year career, Willie played in all 162 games—never missing one of them.

Willie was a great guy to be around. Hornung called him Doctor Feelgood. But when it came to football, he was serious. He hit hard and made big plays. He recovered 21 opponents' fumbles throughout his career. Davis was so quick off the football that offensive tackles had a hard time blocking him. He was selected to play in five consecutive Pro Bowls and was captain of our defense when we won our first championship in 1961.

Forrest Gregg (1956, 1958–1970)
Tackle, Guard 6'4", 249 lbs. (Southern Methodist)
1956, 1958–1970 Green Bay Packers, 1971 Dallas Cowboys
HOF Class of 1986

Forrest was the Packers' No. 2 draft pick in 1956. He was slotted into the offensive right tackle position as soon as he arrived in Green Bay.

At 6'4" and 249 pounds, Gregg was considered undersized at his position at tackle, but his determination, dedication, and athleticism made up for it.

During an interview, Lombardi once said, "Forrest Gregg is the finest player I ever coached."

If nothing else, he was definitely the most durable player, playing in 187 consecutive games during his 14 seasons with Green Bay. When injuries plagued the Packers' offensive line in 1961 and 1965, Gregg switched to guard to fill the void. In 1964 he replaced injured left guard Fuzzy Thurston, and in 1967, Gregg filled in at right guard for Jerry Kramer. That same year he was named All-Pro at guard in one poll and All-Pro at tackle in another. Between 1959 and 1968, Gregg was selected to play in nine Pro Bowls.

According to Paul Hornung, "Gregg was our best offensive lineman and maybe even the best all-around athlete on the team. Lombardi loved him because he always did everything exactly as he said. The coaches had certain criteria they used to grade the offensive linemen, and Forrest always graded high."

He was as good a teammate as one could ever hope to have. Like many of us, he was unselfish and only cared about the good of the team and winning.

Paul Hornung (1957–1962, 1964–1966)
Halfback 6'2", 215 lbs. (Notre Dame)
1957–1962, 1964–1966 Green Bay Packers
HOF Class of 1986

They called him Golden Boy. His curly locks, good looks, and swashbuckling style—not to mention his Heisman Trophy athletic ability—made him one of the best football players and playboys in the country in the 1950s and 1960s. Producers in Hollywood were impressed with his looks and gave him bit parts and cameo roles in movies. He knew all the beautiful women and received so much female fan mail that he hired a friend to take care of it.

This former quarterback at South Bend and halfback for Lombardi's Packers was one of the biggest stars and one of the finest players on the roster. He also got into the worst trouble.

Hornung's reputation of late-night curfew violations, endless parties with power-drinking teammates, and beautiful women at every NFL port of call are well known and documented. Jerry Kramer remembered one such incident. He said, "I remember one game early in my career where we needed to win the ballgame to win the division. I look over and I see Hornung walking through the hotel lobby with a sweet pea on each arm and a martini glass in each hand. This was on Saturday night!

"So I go over there and get in his face. It was very unusual for me to get on Paul's ass, but I felt pretty strong about it. I looked him straight in the eye and said, 'Hey, bud, this ballgame is terribly critical for us, and it doesn't look to me like you're going to be ready for it.' I really challenged his ass.

"He looked straight back at me and said, 'You watch me tomorrow. You watch me inside the 5-yard line. You watch me in short-yardage situations to see if I'm ready or not.'

"So I said, 'Good enough!' The next day, I watched him very closely in those situations. He was great. So that's when I learned that Paul came to 1:00 differently from the rest of us, but he always showed up ready to play."

Jim Ringo recalled an incident that occurred while playing the Rams in Los Angeles in 1957. He said, "On Sunday, December 8, 1957, we were playing the Rams at the Coliseum in Los Angeles. The Packers defense was on the field, and our offense was either standing around on the sideline or sitting on the bench. One of those guys on the bench was Hornung. All of a sudden, a good-looking blonde woman approached Paul on the bench and asked if she could have her picture taken with the Golden Boy, and this was while the game was in progress! It was an extremely bold move on her part, but Paul, being Paul, stood and posed for a photo with her! Unbelievable!"

Paul and his partner in crime, Max McGee, continually tried Lombardi's patience. Coach would say, "You go ahead and test me. It's going to cost you both a lot of money!" And it did. The fine money that Lombardi collected each year was used for a postseason party for players and coaches. Paul says the events were known as the McGee and Hornung parties.

Hornung always had great stories to tell. He told this one about McGee, Lombardi, and himself. "Unlike the rest of the Packers, I was never scared of Lombardi, even though I argued with him constantly," he said. "I never won a single argument, although I know—and he knew—that I was right many times.

"Once, when we were in training camp, he was watching film when he got a call from his wife.

"'Happy anniversary, shithead,' she said.

"Lombardi had forgotten his wedding anniversary, and it put him in such a foul mood that he decided to take bed check himself. He rarely took bed check, usually leaving it to his assistant coaches.

"We heard him coming, so Max and I quickly put our beds together and took off all our clothes. When Lombardi opened the door, Max and I were locked in an embrace.

"'Please, Coach,' I said, 'would you close the door and leave us alone?'

"Lombardi was dumbfounded. He backed out of the room and closed the door. Then he stood out in the hallway until he finally bellowed, 'What's going on in there? I'm coming in!'

"This time Max and I were laughing so hard we were almost crying. Lombardi finally understood that he'd been had. He said, 'What am I going to do with you two?'

"But at least he had forgotten his foul mood."

Lombardi wasn't the only authority figure Paul had a problem with. Following the Packers' second-straight title in 1962, NFL commissioner Pete Rozelle suspended Hornung for the entire 1963 season for gambling. Paul openly admits to betting on NFL games and says that gambling among players in the league was fairly rampant. But Rozelle felt it was in the best interest of the NFL's image to suspend one of its biggest celebrities rather than risk him appearing before a Senate subcommittee hearing.

Due to injuries, Paul didn't play in Super Bowl I. Before the next season, he was selected in the expansion draft by New Orleans, but he retired with arm and vertebrae problems before ever playing a down for the Saints.

In nine seasons, Hornung scored 760 points on 62 touchdowns, 190 PATs; and 66 field goals. He rushed for 3,711 yards and added a total of 1,480 yards on pass receptions.

Even though the Green Bay Packers had quality players at almost every position during the "dynasty years" of the 1960s, many insist that Hornung was the most important contributor to the Packers' successes. He was above all a leader to whom the Packers looked for the big plays in the big games.

Henry Jordan (1959–1969)
Defensive Tackle 6'2", 248 lbs. (Virginia)
1957–1958 Cleveland Browns, 1959–1969 Green Bay Packers
HOF Class of 1995

Henry Jordan began his pro football career as a fifth-round draft pick of the 1957 Cleveland Browns. While with Cleveland, Henry established himself as a hard-hitting defensive tackle, but before the 1959 season, the Browns sent him to the Packers for a fourth-round draft choice.

He proved to be a key player in Lombardi's program. While Adderley and Wood intimidated rival pass receivers with their quickness and aggressiveness, Henry Jordan teamed with Willie Davis to give us two of the best pass rushers in the league. Henry was quick and played smart. His specialization was in putting pressure on the quarterback. Offensive linemen hated to block Henry because he was even quicker than Davis.

Jordan won All-NFL acclaim five times in 1960, 1961, 1962, 1963, and 1964 and also played in four Pro Bowls, seven NFL title games, and Super Bowls I and II. He was the fifth defensive player from the Packers to be elected to the Pro Football Hall of Fame behind lineman Willie Davis, linebacker Ray Nitschke, cornerback Herb Adderley, and safety Willie Wood.

Ray Nitschke (1958–1972)
Middle Linebacker 6'3", 235 lbs. (Illinois)
1958–1972 Green Bay Packers
HOF Class of 1978

According to quarterback and teammate Bart Starr, "Ray Nitschke was a classic example of Dr. Jekyll and Mr. Hyde. Off the field he was a thoughtful, caring person. On the field, he was a ferocious middle linebacker who at times seemed to truly enjoy hitting people."

Nitschke was the most beloved, feared, and dominant player in Green Bay's long and storied history. The typical die-hard football fan was familiar with Ray's intimidating persona—his four front teeth were missing, there wasn't one hair on his head, and his eyes were blackened.

One season he bled consistently from a cut on the center of his forehead that caused blood to drip down over his face the entire game. Opposing quarterbacks would look across and see Nitschke bleeding under his face mask. It got them thinking that the next blood shed might be theirs!

Ray was born in Elmwood Park, Illinois, but grew up in Cicero, a tough Chicago suburb. He was raised by his older brother, and the two of them were tough guys who didn't mind getting into bar fights. They didn't always win. After we won the 1961 NFL championship, the Nitschke brothers got the shit beat out of them by two of Ray's teammates, Dan Currie and Bill Quinlan. It wasn't over anything in particular—just a bunch of drunk jocks blowing off steam after a big win.

When Ray was in high school, he made All-State as a quarterback and had the option of signing a professional baseball contract with the St. Louis Browns. Instead, he opted for a football scholarship at Illinois, where he played fullback on offense and linebacker on defense. It was at Illinois where Ray lost his four front teeth. The Illini were playing Ohio State in 1956, and at the time face masks were not mandatory. Players could show their toughness by going without. A guard hit him on a kickoff, and the four teeth were gone. Ray described the aftermath, saying, "During a timeout, somebody shoved a wad of cotton in my mouth, and I went on with the game, spitting blood all over the field."

When Ray was initially drafted by the Packers in 1958 as their No. 3 draft choice, he was somewhat disappointed. Hailing from Chicago, and having played for Illinois, he had always dreamed of playing for the Bears. Nevertheless, Ray took his $500 signing bonus, spent $300 of it on a used Pontiac, and drove to Green Bay. And for the record, Nitschke took the remaining $200 and gave it to a family whose house he used to eat Sunday dinners at while he attended Illinois.

For the first few years that Nitschke and I were teammates, Ray was a real pain, but when he finally decided to give up alcohol he turned into one of the greatest players of all. To his dying day—March 8, 1998—Packers fans loved him. So did his teammates. Paul Hornung had many good Nitschke stories:

> The thousand-yard rushers from the previous year were honored at Fuzzy Thurston's restaurant, The Left Guard, in Appleton. Rick Casares from the Chicago Bears was there.

Ray walked in, and all Casares wanted was for Nitschke to say one thing to him. He was going to get him. So the first thing Nitschke says to Casares is, "Hey, Rick, congratulations. I heard you married that rich broad from Tampa."

That was all Casares needed to hear. He asked Ray to repeat himself and then said, "You are a real asshole, Nitschke, and I want you to come outside with me because I'm going to teach you a lesson."

Ray was one of the toughest guys in the league, but he wasn't in Rick's class. Hell, in Chicago, even Doug Atkins, the ferocious All-Pro defensive end and one of the meanest men in the league, wouldn't mess with Rick. I knew that if they went outside, Casares would hurt Ray and hurt him bad.

So I stopped the fight before it started, even though Casares kept taunting and abusing Nitschke. He hurt him as badly with his mouth as he would have with his fists. He humiliated Ray, who took it without saying a word. But as I told Nitschke later, not kidding, "What you don't understand is that I saved your life that day."

I remember another time when we arrived in Los Angles for a game against the Rams. In those days, the coaches and the players went to separate bars to drink. It was an unwritten rule that the two would always be separate. On this trip, Nitschke and some others went to a little place in Santa Monica where I knew the owner.

Ray was sitting at the bar by himself, which was a no-no. He was drinking in the daytime, which was another no-no. Then, damned if Lombardi and other coaches didn't come in, a violation of the unspoken agreement between coaches and players.

Instead of paying his check and sliding out of there, Nitschke, the dumb SOB, sent the coaches a beer. When Lombardi saw him, he went ballistic. "Get out, goddammit! You're suspended!" yelled Lombardi. I thought he was going to kick Ray off the team right then and there.

Once he cooled off, Lombardi realized we might not win the game without the best linebacker in the NFL. So, cleverly, he put the Nitschke question up to the team, knowing we sure as hell wouldn't vote to kick him off.

"As far as I'm concerned, we'll do without him," Lombardi said. "It's not fair to you guys if I let him get away with this. I'm going to leave this room and let you guys vote."

When Lombardi was gone, I raised my hand and said, "I vote to kick him off the team and send his ass back to Chicago."

Everybody laughed but Nitschke, who wasn't amused.

"Goddammit, Hornung," he said. "I'm going to kick your ass."

He was still mad even after we had voted to keep him on!

Ray got his revenge in practice. Every Tuesday, we'd have blitz-pickup drills. That meant the backs were supposed to pick up the linebackers and block them. I wasn't in helmet and pads, but every play Nitschke would hit me hard with his forearm. I finally had enough. "You hit me with that forearm again," I said, "and I'm coming after that knee of yours!"

Lombardi blew the whistle and stopped the drill. But the next Tuesday, I came out fully dressed in helmet and pads. When Lombardi asked me what was going on, I said, "I'm not gonna stand here and let him run over me like that. If he's going to hit me, I'm going to protect myself."

And that was the end of that.

Jerry Kramer remembered another Nitschke story. "Nitschke didn't want to go against a rookie player in a practice drill. That is, until the rookie called Nitschke a 'sonofabitch.' Ray then knocked the man unconscious with a single forearm."

In Ray's mind, Lombardi was more than human, he was almost supernatural. Ray reminisced about two of the jokes players used to crack about the Italian bulldog from Brooklyn. "A football player who died and went to heaven noticed a team of angels scrimmaging while a short fellow stood on the sideline yelling at them. The player asked St. Peter, 'Who's that?' St. Peter replied, 'Oh, that's God. He thinks he's Vince Lombardi.'"

Another had to do with his wife, Marie: "One winter night Coach Lombardi got into bed and his wife, Marie, said, 'God, your feet are cold!' Lombardi answered, 'Around home, dear, you can call me Vince.'"

Jim Ringo (1953–1963)
Center 6'2", 232 lbs. (Syracuse)
1953–1963 Green Bay Packers, 1964–1967 Philadelphia Eagles
HOF Class of 1981

Jim Ringo was drafted out of Syracuse and was our center from 1953 to 1963. When he first arrived at the Packers training camp, he was completely intimidated by what he saw. At 6'2" inches tall and 211 pounds, the other players totally outweighed him. He turned around and went home. He returned to camp after being persuaded by his family.

Lombardi bulked him up to 235 pounds, but even back then, that was still considered small for an offensive lineman. But Jim had speed, quickness, and intelligence, which helped him not only dominate his opponents but also successfully lead our Packers sweep. I am definitely testament to that.

When coach Vince Lombardi took over the Packers in 1959, Jim was the only already-established All-Pro on the roster. Lombardi built his offense around Ringo.

When questioned about Jim's size, Vince told the press, "A bigger man might not be able to make the cutoff blocks on our sweeps the way Jim does. The reason Ringo's the best in the league is because he's quick and he's smart."

After seven Pro Bowl honors and two NFL championships, Jim was traded to the Philadelphia Eagles.

Bart Starr (1956–1971)
Quarterback 6'1", 197 lbs. (Alabama)
1956–1971 Green Bay Packers
HOF Class of 1977

He was one of the most perfect men I've ever met. He was poised and very much the perfectionist in everything he did. His leadership was second to none.

Bart's locker was located next to Paul Hornung's, and during all the years I knew him, I never heard him curse. Besides, Paul swore enough for the entire team!

After a decent career on some bad pre–Bear Bryant Alabama teams, Bart was the 200th pick in the 1956 NFL draft. At Green Bay, coaches

Blackbourn and McLean used him as a backup. Three years later, his playing time was still limited and his football future appeared doubtful. That's when Vince Lombardi took over as the Packers' coach, an event that may have saved Bart's NFL career.

He finally moved into the starting lineup in 1960. That same year Starr led Green Bay to the Western Division championship, the first in a long string of successes for him and the Packers. From 1960 through 1967, Bart's win-loss record was an incredible 73–22–4 as the Packers won six division titles, five NFL championships, and the first two Super Bowls. Bart would remain the Packers' quarterback until his retirement following the 1971 season.

One of the great myths about being an NFL quarterback is that it's imperative to have a strong arm. As Bart proved, that's simply not true. How far you throw the ball isn't nearly as important as how accurate and smart you are.

Starr would listen to and count on what his offensive linemen had to say to him. If one of them told Bart that he could dominate his defensive opponent and block him either left or right, Bart would take him at his word. But the lineman had better be able to do what he said he could, or he'd have to answer to Bart.

Willie Wood (1960–1971)
Safety 6'0", 190 lbs. (Southern California)
1960–1971 Green Bay Packers
HOF Class of 1989

Willie Wood was a University of Southern California quarterback who specialized in running the ball and was not drafted by any National Football League team. With a strong desire to play professional football, Willie sent postcards to several NFL teams asking for a tryout. Lombardi liked this sort of initiative, so he decided to take a look. And that's how the Packers got a guy who turned out to be the best free safety in the league, an eight-time Pro Bowl player, and a member of the Pro Football Hall of Fame.

Willie had a good, strong arm, but there was no way he was going to beat out Bart Starr in Lombardi's system. So he didn't complain when Lombardi asked him to try out for the free safety position.

Coach was particularly impressed with Willie's vertical leaping ability. Wood could dunk the football over the crossbar of the goalposts with ease.

Willie was also a tough player and would tackle anyone—regardless of size. He would play with pain if necessary. He said, "Once I had hurt my shoulder so badly that it almost brought me to tears. When I was asked if I wanted to go to the sideline, I responded with, 'No, I'm OK. I've got another shoulder.'"

In his first start against Baltimore in 1960, Willie was up against Johnny Unitas and Raymond Berry. He remembered, "Unitas picked on me right from the start. He rifled two touchdown passes to Berry. I was scared just to guard Ray. I thought my pro career was at an end. I figured my mistakes cost us the game—that is, until Norb Hecker, our defensive backfield coach, gave me a vote of confidence. He told me that those things happen and to forget it. He was right."

In 1961 Willie led the league with a 16.1-yard average on punt returns, and in 1962 he led the league with nine interceptions. Along with Max McGee and Bart Starr, he played a starring role in Super Bowl I in 1967, intercepting a Lenny Dawson pass and returning it 50 yards to the Chiefs' five. On the following play, Elijah Pitts took it in for the score, and we defeated the Chiefs 35–10.

Willie retired following the 1971 season.

The Rest of the Guys
Max McGee (1954–1967)
End 6'3", 205 lbs. (Tulane)
1954–1967 Green Bay Packers

Max wasn't your typical Lombardi player. He was well known for his all-night partying and infamous late-night escapade the night before we played the Chiefs in Super Bowl I. It has been said that former Packers great and Hall of Famer Johnny Blood McNally would have been proud of McGee's legendary tales.

McGee will always be remembered as the player who caught the first touchdown pass in Super Bowl history as we defeated Kansas City 35–10 in Super Bowl I in 1967.

Emlen Tunnell (1959–1961)
Defensive Back 6'1", 187 lbs. (Toledo, Iowa)
1948–1958 New York Giants, 1959–1961 Green Bay Packers
HOF Class of 1967

While playing football at Iowa, Emlen Tunnell suffered a broken neck. His injury was so severe that both the army and navy refused to sign him up. Tunnell, wanting to do his part for the armed forces, was finally accepted to enlist with the coast guard.

Emlen returned to the University of Iowa following his coast guard service but left after the 1947 season. Many of the professional football teams thought that Tunnell would play a third year at Iowa; therefore, he was not drafted in 1948.

In 1948 Emlen, a free agent, contacted the New York Giants and asked for a tryout with the team. They liked what they saw and offered him a contract. He was offered the position of defensive back.

In 1959 Tunnell was traded to Green Bay at Lombardi's request. It was part of Lombardi's strategy to include veteran players who had an understanding of what it took to win.

Emlen was considered a father figure to the young black players on our team. Color didn't matter to him, only that players have the will to play and the desire to win. He helped out guys like Willie Wood who, in 1960, joined the team with a chip on his shoulder.

Tunnell was dubbed the King of Harlem by Hornung. He spent all his time and money there by investing in businesses. He spent his final three years with the Packers.

He became the first black player to play for New York and was also the first black player to be inducted into the Pro Football Hall of Fame. Emlen was enshrined as a New York Giant after spending 11 years with the team.

Bill Quinlan (1959–1962)
Defensive End 6'3", 248 lbs. (Michigan State)
1957–1958 Cleveland Browns, 1959–1962 Green Bay Packers, 1963 Philadelphia Eagles, 1964 Detroit Lions, 1965 Washington Redskins

Another veteran player who was brought in by Lombardi was defensive end Bill Quinlan. Bill was originally drafted by the Cleveland Browns in

1956 but only played two years with the team. Not long after he had been acquired by Green Bay, we found out why Lombardi picked him.

One day after practice, Quinlan got all over the team, saying, "No wonder you guys aren't champions. You don't talk like champions. You talk like you enjoy getting beat."

Then he turned his sights on Dave "Hog" Hanner and said, "You're not smart enough to be an end. You don't have the speed, and you can't diagnose the plays. You're not tough enough. You don't have the ability or the brains."

You could see the smoke coming out of Hanner's ears. He was all ready to knock Bill on his ass and yelled, "OK, Quinlan, let's go outside and settle this!"

Then a smile came over Bill's face, and he said, "That's the way, Dave. Now you're talking like a champion!"

Jerry Kramer (1958–1968)
Guard 6'3", 245 lbs. (Idaho)
1958–1968 Green Bay Packers

Jerry was one of the best blockers in the game. Vince Lombardi was a guard when he played at Fordham and became one of the famous Seven Blocks of Granite. Lombardi said, "The guards are the focal point of the offense. Everything they do is critical. They open the holes for the backs, break the way for the sweeps, and bodyguard the passer.

"As for Kramer, nothing intimidates him. He not only ignores the small hurts but the large ones too. And the evidence of his indifference is all over his body."

In the locker room, Jerry was known as Old Zipperhead. He had broken one of the vertebrae in his neck. An operation was required, and the result was a six-inch scar that ran down his neck. That wasn't all. His right hand was permanently half-clenched due to a shotgun accident. Another time he had broken his ankle, and the doctors had to hold it together with a two-inch pin. He even once played with a retinal detachment!

Despite these setbacks, Kramer was selected as an All-Pro five times—in 1960, 1962, 1963, 1966, and 1967. He was the only guard selected for the NFL's 50th Anniversary All-Time Team and the only member of that team not in the Pro Football Hall of Fame.

Ron Kramer (1957–1964)
End-Tight End 6'3", 234 lbs. (Michigan)
1957–1964 Green Bay Packers, 1965–1967 Detroit Lions

Another great player was Ron Kramer, our tight end. He was such a great athlete that both the Packers and the Detroit Pistons of the NBA drafted him.

Ron was the biggest lineman on our team. An all-around athlete at Michigan, he stood just over 6'3"and weighed more than 230 pounds. He was an All-American in his junior and senior years and top scorer on the Wolverine basketball team for three straight seasons. In track, he was the team's best shot putter and high jumper. Kramer was also the last athlete to achieve nine letters at Michigan.

In 1957 the Packers were the "doormat" of the league. Ron Kramer was the fourth choice in the 1957 draft. That same year the Pack also had a "bonus choice." They used it to select All-American back Paul Horning from Notre Dame. Since both Paul and Ron could claim that they were first-round picks in the 1957 draft, Kramer wanted to set the record straight, saying, "I was Green Bay's 'first' draft choice, and Paul was the first-round 'bonus' draft choice. Back in those days, if a team was on the bottom rung for several years, the league gave them a bonus choice plus their first-round draft choice."

However, Ron's rookie year came to an abrupt end when he suffered leg and knee injuries while catching a pass in a 42–17 loss to the Los Angeles Rams. He said, "I broke my leg and tore up my knee badly in the next-to-last game. The doctors said I should never play again, but after I recouped it, I played another 10 years."

He sat out the 1958 season because he had enlisted into the air force. Ron returned to the Packers in 1959 but did not meet Lombardi's physical criteria. He remembered, "I arrived at Green Bay a week before the 1959 season started, and I was not in shape to play. I weighed 212 pounds, had ulcers, and my health was a mess. It took me a year and a half to get back in shape. But Lombardi told me, 'You're either going to make it, or I'm going to get rid of you.' I said, 'OK, let's have a show of it.' The rest is history."

Lombardi used to refer to Ron as the 12th Man, and Ron said, "I was very proud of that statement. We didn't have to double-team the defensive ends. I could block the end alone. So I was the prototype at tight end."

In 1961 Kramer became the league's best tight end. Ron was a hell of a blocker and an excellent receiver. He was twice selected as All-Pro.

Fred (Fuzzy) Thurston (1959–1967)
Guard 6'1", 247 lbs. (Valparaiso)
1956 Philadelphia Eagles, 1957 Chicago Bears, 1958 Baltimore Colts, 1959–1967 Green Bay Packers

Drafted by the Eagles in 1956, Thurston bounced from the Eagles to the Bears to the Colts before he found a home with the Packers in 1959.

Thurston may have been smaller than right guard Jerry Kramer, but he was chunkier. The left guard teamed up with Kramer to form the perfect guard tandem for Lombardi's run to daylight offense.

Kramer remembered Fuzzy fondly and said, "I always told people that Fuzzy was like a 5-year-old on Christmas morning who gets a box of horse shit for Christmas, and he's jumping up and down and going, 'Yippee.' And somebody asks him, 'What are you celebrating?' And Fuzzy says, where there's horse shit, there's got to be a pony around here someplace.'"

Fuzzy will always be remembered by Packers fans for his response to a sportswriter's question when asked how he prepared for the Ice Bowl, played in temperatures that were 15 degrees below. Without hesitation, Fuzzy said, "About 10 vodkas!"

When asked to share his best piece of advice, Fuzzy always replied, "Never, never quit until it's over. You've always got a chance."

Lombardi definitely left an impact on Thurston. After calling the legendary coach a brilliant man, Thurston quickly added, "But he scared the hell out of me."

To this day, Fuzzy continues to live on Lombardi time, always showing up 15 minutes early for every appointment.

From Green Bay to New Orleans

Chapter  37

The Beginning of the End

In April 1967, Dallas Cowboys coach Tom Landry made an astonishing prediction at a speaking engagement in St. Paul, Minnesota. He predicted that one of the other teams would "displace" the Packers within two years. Landry continued, "They are approaching an age problem, and other teams are improving."

Landry's prediction proved correct, and the Packers were displaced within two years. Green Bay's reign ended in 1968 with Super Bowl II. They would not return as world champions until Super Bowl XXXI in 1997.

In 1967 the Packers were the oldest team in the NFL. Ten of our players were at their 10th-season mark and others were close to it. But Lombardi was determined to win an unprecedented third consecutive championship—regardless of the fact that teams such as the Cowboys, Rams, and Colts now had the talent to compete with the Packers.

At the conclusion of the 1966 season, I had played out my option to become a free agent. The Packers had signed running backs Donny Anderson out of Texas Tech and Jim Grabowski out of Illinois for a hell of a lot more money than any of the veterans were making. Lombardi insisted that it was a necessary move to keep the AFL from acquiring all the good, young players.

I know that Lombardi had asked Hornung to speak to me about this matter at least several times or more, but nothing was going to make me change my mind. There was no way those two guys should have been getting more than the established veteran stars. At the end of the '65 season I had insisted to Lombardi that he give me a three-year contract at $75,000 per year. Lombardi countered with a one-year contract for $75,000. Throughout the 1966 season, he tried to convince me to sign, but I remained adamant in my stance.

Though we didn't realize it at the time, our championship Packers team had begun to break up. Ron Kramer was traded to Detroit, Fuzzy Thurston was out for the season with an injury, and Forrest Gregg had retired and was an assistant coach with Tennessee. It would be the last year that the future Hall of Fame members—Hornung, Starr, Jordan, Davis, Adderley, Wood, Nitschke, and me—would play together.

It was at this time that Paul was plagued with arm, neck, and back injuries that developed over his years of playing football. He could no longer play the game the way he had earlier in his career. He was in so much pain that he declined to play in the first NFL-AFL World Championship Game in Los Angeles. The year 1967 saw the addition of an expansion team in Louisiana called the New Orleans Saints, and rumors began to surface that Lombardi was going to put Hornung on the list for the New Orleans expansion draft.

This is how the Saints acquired their players. Each NFL team was required to submit 11 names. After the Saints picked one player from each team, they returned the lists to the teams, who then could withdraw two names before resubmitting the list for the second round of the draft.

Some felt that Saints coach Tom Fears would not sign Paul because of his injuries, while others thought that Lombardi would not trade him—but Coach saw this as a smart business move.

Lombardi was sad and apologetic to Paul when he told him that he had put his name on the list. Hornung was already one step ahead. He had already worked out a deal, in secret, with minority owner Bedford Wynne for $1 million for three years. The most he had ever made with the Packers was about $80,000. When the expansion draft was held, Paul became one of the first New Orleans Saints players.

The second round had yet to be conducted, and Paul was asked about the possibility that I might join him in New Orleans. Hornung knew that I was still very angry with Lombardi regarding the money that Grabowski and Anderson had signed for. I knew that with Paul gone and both backs lacking in experience, Lombardi would want me for at least one more year. But it was not to be.

On July 6, after nine seasons with the Packers—during which I set a club record of 8,207 yards rushing—I signed with the Saints, and the Packers received a first-round draft choice. I would play the 1967 season in New Orleans—my final year in professional football.

Signing with the Saints was more ceremonial than anything else. It was the franchise's inaugural year with the NFL and I became one of its biggest draws. Being from Louisiana, it was not only a natural move but a smart one as well. I had played at LSU, was the Louisiana kid who had made it big in the frozen tundra of the north for the world champion Packers, and received more money than Lombardi was willing to pay. Part of the deal was that Hornung and I would tour the state together to drum up interest and sell tickets for the new franchise.

After Paul had signed with the team, Tom Fears told the media, "Hornung has a lot of good football left in him. It was worth the risk."

But Tom and Paul were dead wrong. After reviewing Paul's x-rays at Scripps Medical Center in San Diego, a doctor told him that he would have to retire immediately or take the risk of having one hit turn him into a paraplegic.

That was all Paul needed to hear. He told the Saints the reasons behind his decision to retire, then immediately flew out to Hollywood to announce his retirement on the *Johnny Carson Show*. Typical Hornung style.

Chapter

1967 New Orleans Saints— the Inaugural Year

On All Saints Day, November 1, 1966, New Orleans was awarded the NFL's 16th franchise. Atlanta Falcons offensive coordinator Tom Fears was named head coach. Prior to working for the Falcons, Tom had been on staff at Green Bay and Los Angeles.

The Saints had signed some big names to their roster. Quarterback Billy Kilmer and defensive end Doug Atkins were just a few of the Saints' stars picked from the expansion draft list.

Even with the big names, the Saints still had a few kinks in their armor that needed to be corrected. For example, 10 minutes into our first practice, the equipment managers realized that they forgot to order footballs. Oh, well, just a minor oversight, I guess.

Our new franchise actually started off quite well. The preseason posted a 5–1 record—the best ever for a first-year expansion team. Our only loss was to the Rams in Anaheim.

Vince Lombardi, who was an early advocate of isometric exercises and other conditioning, strains at the pulley as I guide the 10 with my thumb at the Packers training camp on September 2, 1965. Photo courtesy of AP Images.

Paul Hornung—one of my best friends on the team—and I watch the action from the sideline during this 1966 game. Photo courtesy of Getty Images.

Me during a tough battle against the Cleveland Browns in the NFL Championship Game on January 2, 1966. Photo courtesy of Getty Images.

Here I am running with a Bart Starr pass as Dallas Cowboy Mel Renfro (No. 20) leaps high in air too late to break up the pass during the 1966 NFL Championship Game on January 1, 1967, in Dallas, TX. We defeated the Cowboys 34–27. Photo courtesy of AP Images.

Max McGee and I take the field during one of the most historically significant events in football history: Super Bowl I on January 15, 1967. The Packers decimated the Kansas City Chiefs 35–10. Photo courtesy of AP Images.

Here I am following Fuzzy Thurston (No. 63) after taking a handoff from Bart Starr (No. 15) during Super Bowl I. Photo courtesy of AP Images.

NBC's George Ratterman (far left) and CBS's Pat Summerall (far right) share the microphone when interviewing Bart Starr and me following our 35–10 victory over the Kansas City Chiefs in Super Bowl I. Photo courtesy of Getty Images.

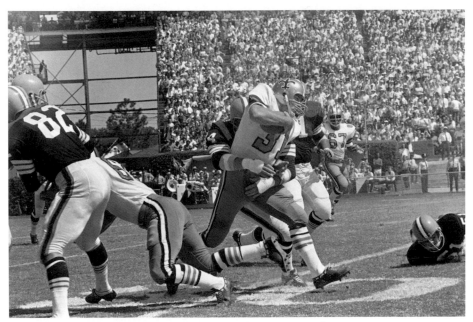

After my long Packers career, I briefly played for the New Orleans Saints. Here I am running for short yardage after pulling in a Bill Kilmer pass against the Cleveland Browns on October 1, 1967, in New Orleans. Photo courtesy of AP Images.

Being inducted into the Pro Football Hall of Fame with the class of 1976. Marie Lombardi was my presenter. Photo courtesy of the author.

Getting to meet and have dinner with George and Barbara Bush was an honor for Helen and me. Photo courtesy of the author.

The three Taylor boys. Clockwise, from left: Webb, Clark, and me. Photo courtesy of the author.

Fellow Hall of Famer Bobby Bell and I compete in the NFL's competition to locate the loudest snorer of all time before Super Bowl XXXVIII in Houston. In the end, the great Jerry Rice proclaimed me the winner. Photo courtesy of the author.

Enjoying a medieval feast with friends at Bunratty Castle in Shannon, Ireland. Helen and I are the king and queen. Photo courtesy of the author.

Christmas 2009 with the Taylors. Top row, left to right: my daughter JoBeth, Helen, me, my son Chip, and my grandson Trey. Bottom row: my granddaughters Erin, Lauren, and Jessica. Photo courtesy of the author.

It was an honor to escort the Tiffany & Co. Vince Lombardi Trophy through the Pro Football Hall of Fame after it was delivered by a Brinks armored car on September 28, 2009, in Canton, Ohio. The trophy remained on display in the Lamar Hunt Super Bowl Gallery throughout the season before being presented to the Super Bowl XLIV winners, the New Orleans Saints, on February 7, 2010, in Miami. Photo courtesy of AP Images.

On September 17, 1967, the Saints took the field for our first regular-season game in front of 80,879 fans at Tulane Stadium against the Los Angeles Rams. We started off with a bang as our rookie receiver John Gilliam returned the opening kickoff 94 yards for a touchdown. But when the final gun sounded, we had lost the game 27–13.

Saints legend has it that following Gilliam's opening kickoff TD, a fan shouted out, "This is going to be the greatest team in history!" thus jinxing the Saints forever.

We continued our consecutive losing streak by succumbing to the Redskins, Browns, Giants, Cowboys, 49ers, and Steelers.

Our first regular-season win finally came during Week 8, when rookie wide receiver Walt Roberts scored three touchdowns against the Eagles. Final score: Saints 31, Eagles 24.

Next we lost to the Cowboys and Eagles but beat the Falcons 27–24, giving us a 2–9 record. We went on to another two-game losing streak—with defeats coming at the hands of the Cardinals and Colts—but we were victorious 30–14 in our final game against the Washington Redskins.

We ended up with a 3–11 record, which really wasn't that bad. Our three wins tied the record for most wins by a first-year expansion franchise.

I led the team with 390 yards rushing and two TDs, while the surprise of the year—17th-round draft pick rookie Danny Abramowicz from Xavier College—led in receiving with 50 catches for a total of 721 yards and six touchdowns. Defensive back Dave Whitsell made the Pro Bowl while leading the NFL in interceptions with 10—still a team record.

At the end of the 1967 season, I retired from professional football. I ended my career with 8,597 yards, 83 rushing touchdowns, and five straight 1,000-yard rushing seasons from 1960 to 1964. I also caught 225 passes for 1,756 yards and 10 touchdowns, and returned seven kickoffs for 185 yards, giving me a total of 10,538 net yards and 93 touchdowns.

New Orleans Saints News Release—Jim Taylor Retires

JIM TAYLOR RETIRES
FOR RELEASE 10:00 AM TUESDAY, SEPTEMBER 10, 1968

The New Orleans Saints Tuesday announced the retirement from active playing status of fullback Jimmy Taylor, who will probably go down in history as Louisiana's greatest football player.

"It is with deep regret and a sense of great loss that Taylor's long playing career has come to an end," said Saints president John W. Mecom Jr. But it perhaps is fitting that he played out his career in his home state of Louisiana where he gave leadership and stability to Louisiana's first professional football team.

Taylor will continue his association with the Saints in a front-office capacity and will function in the area of public relations. He will bring to this new position the knowledge of 10 seasons in the National Football

League. And he will thereby continue to be associated with his fans all over the state.

"Taylor's contribution to the first-year Saints will never be forgotten," said Mecom. "His magnificent efforts with a young, untested team of veterans and rookies were matched only by the leadership and balance he gave the Saints when it was needed the most. We will now count upon him to continue to help the Saints in the same spirit that made him one of Louisiana's most beloved football players."

Taylor, who'll be 33 on September 20, fulfilled a longtime wish of playing in his home state in 1967 when he played out his option with Green Bay and signed with the Saints. The old pro led Saints rushers with 390 yards on 130 carries and was second in receiving with 38 catches for 251 yards.

He began his NFL career at Green Bay in 1958 after gaining All-American acclaim at LSU. While at Green Bay, he fought his way to become the hero of millions. Taylor became a legend in his lifetime to the football fans of Louisiana. It was this realization that prompted Mecom to give up a No. 1 draft choice and a player for Taylor's services.

At his peak in Green Bay, Taylor was the Associated Press Player of the Year in 1962, won the Jim Thorpe Trophy, and was named the top professional player by a national sports magazine. He scored 19 touchdowns in 1962. No other NFL back has ever scored that many from scrimmage in one season. No other man put together five straight 1,000-yard years running as Taylor did from 1960 to 1964. In title games, no man has gained as many yards rushing or as many yards rushing-receiving combined as Taylor.

Taylor holds down second place in All-Time NFL Rushing (8,597 yards) behind former Cleveland fullback Jimmy Brown.

Whatever he does, Taylor will give it all he has. He knows no other way.

The Saints are proud to count him among the men who've worn the old gold, black, and white with pride.

Chapter

From Player to Front Office

The adjustment from professional football to civilian life was difficult. It was something that no one could prepare me for.

When I had signed my contract in 1968 with John Mecom Jr. and the New Orleans Saints, it was for 20 years. After playing only for their inaugural season and then retiring as a player, I still owed them 19 years of service.

During this time I was approached by many NFL coaches and asked to assistant coach their teams. One of these coaches was Tom Landry. Since my contract stated that I could not work for any other NFL team, Mecom would not release me to assistant coach with the Cowboys. I would have really loved that. Instead, I played out my option with the Saints and wore many hats for the organization.

As a player, my timeline with the team began in July and ended in December; but working in the front office extended that timeline, and I was obligated under contractual agreement to work 12 months out of the year.

In 1969 I became the voice of the Saints along with my then broadcasting partner Al Wester on WWL radio. Several years later, I continued my radio broadcasting, but my broadcasting partner became Bill McColgan.

I was also a professional scout for the Saints organization. My job duties included grading films and writing scouting reports. In 1970 I took a trip to Ole Miss to scout this upstart quarterback. I had heard a lot of good things about him and decided to check him out. I liked what I saw and recommended him to the Saints. They must have seen the same thing I did, as they drafted him in the first round (second overall) of the 1971 NFL Draft. His name was Archie Manning.

Besides being the Saints' color analyst and scout, I also supervised and promoted various golf tournaments for the organization and advanced the games on the road by appearing on radio and television shows. I was the media spokesperson and spoke at civic clubs both locally and around the country. On Saturday nights I hosted team and management dinners while participating in boosting ticket sales and community relations. Whatever job the Saints asked me to do, I did...and that was for 19 years!

During this time I also continued to help run the construction company I formed with my dear friend Norman Samaha in the early 1960s. We were in commercial building and built hospitals, churches, office buildings, prisons, etc. I built a few apartment complexes and other income-producing properties at that time. My older brother Clark, an attorney and real-estate developer, got me interested in development.

When my partner died in the early 1980s, I decided to dissolve the company and move on with my life.

About this same time, my marriage to my first wife Dixie ended. Together we had two children—JoBeth and Chip—who are now grown. I moved from New Orleans back home to Baton Rouge to help take care of my elderly mother. I continued to work for the Saints by commuting from Baton Rouge to New Orleans.

Little did I know that my life would be headed for another big change.

Life After Football

ABC'S Wide World of Sports
Superstars Competition

The Superstars Competition was an all-around sports competition that pitted elite athletes from different sports against one another in a series of athletic events resembling a decathlon. In the original ABC *Wide World of Sports* version of the 1970s, no athlete was permitted to compete in the sport(s) of his or her profession.

Competitors participated in 10 different sporting events, including a 100-yard dash, 800-meter run, obstacle course, weightlifting, bowling, rowing, tennis, bicycle racing, basketball, and swimming. Points were awarded for the position in which the competitor placed in each event. The competitor with the most points at the end of all 10 events was declared the champion.

I got my chance to compete in 1977. In the Men's Preliminary (in which there were four heats), it came down to myself and Peter Snell. When I failed to score a point in the obstacle course and Snell made the final, it became clear. If Floyd Little defeated Snell in the obstacle course final, I would win the overall competition. Little appeared to win, but a penalty at the tires gave the obstacle course and overall win to Snell. That error cost me $5,000 in winnings. I ended up placing an overall second (which still qualified me for the Men's Finals) and pocketed $9,100.

In the Men's Finals, I placed fifth behind Kyle Rote Jr., Dave Casper, Guy Drut, and Peter Snell and was awarded $7,300. I still placed high enough to qualify for the World Superstars Championship. I placed eighth and took home $4,440. Bob Seagren placed first.

It was a great experience, and it proved to me that older guys (I was 41 at the time) could still compete with the best of 'em.

Chapter

The Hall of Fame— a Day I Will Never Forget

JIM TAYLOR
Class of 1976
Fullback 6'0", 214 lbs.
Louisiana State University
1958–1966 Green Bay Packers, 1967 New Orleans Saints

James Charles Taylor...LSU All-America, 1957...Packers' No. 2 draft pick, 1958...1,000-yard rusher five straight years, 1960–1964...Rushed for 8,597 yards, caught 225 passes, amassed 10,539 combined net yards, scored 558 points...Led NFL rushers, scorers, had record 19 TDs rushing, 1962... Excelled in 1962 NFL title game...Ferocious runner, rugged blocker, prime disciple of "run to daylight" doctrine...Born September 20, 1935, in Baton Rouge, Louisiana

Getting "the call" that you have been selected to be enshrined into the Pro Football Hall of Fame is the greatest honor a professional football player can receive. I was notified of this honor in February 1976 and was asked to select a presenter.

On July 24, 1976, Ray Flaherty, Len Ford, and I stood upon the steps of the Hall of Fame in front of a packed audience. Back then Jim Muzzy was the announcer for the event. Jim would first announce the presenter, and then the presenter would announce the enshrinee.

Here is what Jim had to say about my presenter, Marie Lombardi:

> It is particularly fitting that Mrs. Vince Lombardi is serving as the presenter for the first player from the great Packers dynasty team of the 1960s to be inducted into the Pro Football Hall of Fame today.
>
> Her famous husband was inducted in 1971, but Jim Taylor is the first of what is expected to be several stars from the powerhouses Coach Lombardi built in Green Bay to be enshrined. Marie has long been a keen observer of football and she still retains her enthusiasm for the sport with which she was once so associated. She first visited the Hall in 1971 when her husband was enshrined and is making her third trip here to present none other than Jim Taylor. I give you Mrs. Vince Lombardi.

Next, Marie spoke:

> Thank you. Correction, this is my fourth trip to Canton. I want to congratulate the enshrinees and to compliment the Hall of Fame on their fine selection this year, and to thank Jimmy Taylor for making me a part of it. It is truly a highlight for me. About six weeks ago I wasn't sure I could be here because I was in the hospital having a nerve block on my face. It is a terrible thing because it numbs the one side of your face, and your mouth doesn't work too well. And what could be worse for a woman if her mouth doesn't work too well!
>
> It shattered me pretty badly when I knew I just couldn't be here, so I called my son in Seattle and I said, "Vince, you better call Jimmy and tell him I can't go to Canton because I can't speak." He said, "All

right, Mother, if that's what you want." An hour later I called him back and said, "Vince, don't call Jimmy because a big voice up there said to me, 'You better be in Canton, and you better do a good job!'" Well, here I am and I better do a good job or Jimmy may possibly trade me. I also suspect that I am pinch-hitting for that Italian with that big voice who can't be here.

Not everybody knows of those fine records that Jimmy made in Green Bay—those magnificent five years where he gained over 1,000 yards. I know he did because I saw him gain every single one of them. But I have to say, today is the day he will be most proud of because, you see, he is the first—the very first of the great Packer players of what is known as the Lombardi era to be inducted into the Hall of Fame. When I go into the Hall and I see the history of this great National Football League, I realize that the decade of the '60s was really something special. I personally feel that it was professional football's and the Packers' finest hour. It must be a great joy for Jimmy to know that he is the first to reach the top.

As Coach Lombardi used to say, I don't care anything about gimmicks or tricks on offense, you play this game with power, you do what you do best and you do it again, and again, and again. Jimmy Taylor was that power, and Vince used to say, "We had thunder and lightning on the Green Bay Packers, and Jimmy Taylor was that thunder."

I have a tape at home that has an interview with Howard Cosell. Vince is evaluating the players, and he says this about Jimmy, and I quote: "Jim Taylor isn't big for a fullback, but when you bump against him it's like bumping against an iron statue—in fact, he likes that feeling. The thing about Jimmy is that he really likes people. I don't know anyone on the squad that has a greater need or a greater capacity for friendship and understanding than Jim Taylor."

Vince and Jim did have their misunderstandings, but who didn't. There's something I would like to share with you. It's special because it's the only time it happened.

When Vince was sick and in the hospital in Washington, many, many Packer players came to see him. One of those players was Jim Taylor. I went into the room with him, and Vince took his hand. He held it and held it for a very long time. I will never, ever forget the love and understanding that went between those two hands.

Today, our country has a great need for heroes. I have a strong belief that the men sitting here—the men who will be enshrined into the Pro Football Hall of Fame—are today's heroes.

I present to you Jimmy Taylor.

Then it was my turn. I'm not one who feels comfortable talking on stage to thousands of people, so I kept my speech short and sweet. Besides, there was a time limit.

Toastmaster, enshrinees, guests, and fans. I would like to thank a few of those people who influenced me with their leadership, patience, and understanding. First of all, I would like to thank my high school football coach, Claude Harrison, and track coach and trainer, Bat Gourrier, of Baton Rouge High School, who were very instrumental in helping to pave my way to professional football and to the Hall of Fame. Basketball coach Kenner Day was a fine gentleman who gave me the strength and confidence to become an athlete. I certainly admired him. Charles McClendon and Paul Dietzel were my coaches at LSU. They believed in me and gave me the opportunity to play college football. And to my Green Bay Packer teammates of the '60s—to Bart Starr, Ray Nitschke, Jerry Kramer, Paul Hornung, and my good friend Fuzzy Thurston—the teamwork, loyalty, and unity that they created gave me the opportunity to be the type of player that I was. Vince Lombardi molded our ballclub into the championship team that we were.

I would like to say a few words about my late coach, Vince Lombardi. He gave me the admiration, dedication, discipline, and determination to become the kind of football player that he wanted. He not only developed me into a football player, but he developed me into a man.

I would like to thank the Hall of Fame members who voted for me, and the fans of Canton, Ohio. It has been a wonderful week, one that I will cherish and remember forever. Thank you.

Standing on that stage and being honored with the two other great men from the class of 1976—New York Yankees and Boston/Washington Redskins coach Ray Flaherty and Cleveland Browns defensive end Len Ford—was an extremely humbling experience.

It was a day I will never forget.

Chapter

HOF Congratulatory Messages

Congratulations on your outstanding career. Sorry other commitments prevent my attending, but I join with thousands of Saints fans and NFL fans everywhere in wishing you the same degree of success in the future as you have enjoyed in professional football.

—Pete Rozelle, Commissioner of Professional Football

Please accept the congratulations of the Professional Football Hall of Fame on Jim Taylor Day in New Orleans. Your contributions to pro football have been outstanding, and all who have seen you play will never forget the quality of your sterling performances. Our best wishes to you in the future.

—Dick Gallagher, Director, Professional Football Hall of Fame

Congratulations and best wishes to the National Football League's greatest fullback. Good luck in the future.

—Vince Lombardi Jr., Green Bay Packers

As teammates of Jim Taylor for nine seasons and four world titles, the Green Bay Packers all salute the great fullback whose fiery determination and second effort was an inspiration to all. Best wishes to Jim and his family.

—Willie Davis and Bob Skoronski, Cocaptains, World Champion Green Bay Packers

We are happy to join with the other NFL clubs in paying tribute to an outstanding football player on his day. The Cardinals have always felt that you were a key factor in many championships. Best wishes for the future.

—Bill Bidwill, Vice President, St. Louis Cardinals

Congratulations to a great football player. Your record of 10 years in the National Football League with 93 touchdowns—some of them acquired in combat with our Bears—establishes you as one of the greatest backs in modern football history.

We of the Chicago Bears salute you, Jim Taylor, for your achievements to professional football and for your sportsmanship throughout your career.

—George S. Halas, Chicago Bears

The Minnesota Vikings are pleased to join with all clubs in the National Football League in wishing you well on this special day. Your many seasons as an outstanding player have not only brought pleasure to football fans throughout the country, but have served to strengthen the growth of the National Football League. Congratulations, Jim, on a job well done.

—Jim Finks, General Manager, Minnesota Vikings

The San Francisco 49ers wish to join with your many NFL friends in extending best wishes on this occasion. We only wish you had decided to retire while you were still in the Western Conference.

—Lou Spadia, San Francisco 49ers

Jim Taylor's records alone stand as a monument to the man. Congratulations!

—The Pittsburgh Steelers

Through your years in retirement, the Baltimore Colts wish you all of the success you enjoyed as one of the finest fullbacks pro football has ever known.

—Don Shula, Baltimore Colts

Chapter

My Sky Goddess

In the mid-1980s, I met my current wife, the former Helen Spillman. Helen had moved back home to Baton Rouge from Houston to be closer to her elderly parents. We got to know each other while riding the Lifecycle exercise bikes at our health club and were good friends for a year or so before we began dating. It wasn't too long before we realized that we were right for each other.

We were married on May 5, Cinco de Mayo. We honeymooned in Paris and along the French Riviera, which was absolutely fabulous! On our first anniversary, we had the chance to experience a *real* Cinco de Mayo in Acapulco. Our marriage was off to a good start!

Helen and I were both physical education majors at LSU and love all sports. Helen also attended grad school at LSU for exercise physiology. Sports and traveling have made our lives fun. My Sky Goddess (as I call her) is always planning something adventurous for us to do. One minute I'm sitting at home, and the next I'm on a plane to see LSU win the National Baseball Championship in Omaha, Nebraska, or in Indianapolis to see the men's Final Four in basketball.

We also enjoy traveling to some of the most naturally beautiful destinations in the world. Some of our favorites have been the Rancho Le Puerto in Mexico; Red Mountain Resort in St. George, Utah; Canyon Ranch in Tucson; and the Berkshires. We love to hike in the mountains and cycle the canyons. We've also heard the Vienna Boys Choir sing in Vienna; toured Prague, Budapest, Ireland, Spain, Germany, Switzerland, Brazil, Chile, and Argentina; and have traveled extensively throughout France and Italy.

In 2006 Helen surprised me with a trip to New York for the NFL Draft at Radio City Music Hall. From trips to Yellowstone National Park to eating lobster on the beach in Maine to riding the cable cars in San Francisco, there is never a dull moment with Helen. We are always exploring some new, uncharted territory.

Running is another passion we both share. He have run numerous 5K and 10K races, and I have trained for and run a marathon. The Vince Lombardi 5K Run to Daylight race in Milwaukee and the world's largest 10K—the Peachtree Road Race—in Atlanta, Georgia, are two of our favorites.

Helen and I also enjoy attending LSU football games and pulling for our alma mater. We have a group of friends who we tailgate and watch the games with. We even sat with the LSU athletic director and chancellor at the Sugar Bowl and Peach Bowl, SEC Championship Games, and BCS National Championship Games while we cheered our Fighting Tigers to victory. Helen and I are also very active with the LSU Booster Club. We attend many of the college functions that help raise money for athletics and academics.

We love to attend Packers and Saints alumni weekends, where we get to visit with many of our old friends. Each year the stories get better and better! We were in New Orleans to see Green Bay win its last Super Bowl and in Miami to see the Saints win their first.

At the time I met her, Helen was an international flight attendant with Delta Airlines. She loved what she did, and it showed in the many wonderful letters about her that passengers sent to Delta. Because of her kindness and wonderful service, she has been the recipient of three plaques for her services, and in 2001 Helen received one of Delta's highest honors. Out of more than 80,000 Delta employees, 100 men and women were selected by their peers as tops in their field.

We both feel that we have met our soul mate and enjoy each and every day together. Whether we are home barbequing in the backyard or on some new adventure, we look at life as a true gift from God. Helen and I have made the most of it, and we will continue to do so together.

Chapter

The Worst Day of My Life

Throughout my pro football career, I was hit, slammed, pounced on, and thrown to the ground. I'd always been able to shake it off and keep on playing, but on the morning of June 3, 2004, I was unexpectedly struck down by an insidious opponent that could neither be seen nor heard. It not only paralyzed me but also forced me to become a prisoner in my own body.

For years I had been a paragon of health, eating and exercising properly and keeping my weight around 206 to 208 pounds. But on the morning of June 3, none of that mattered. That morning I was taking my daily five-to-six-mile walk, when all of a sudden my arm crimped up and I was limping. Paralysis had already set in. I tried to get to neutral ground to sit down. I knew I was in trouble. I had no motor skills or strength and fell back on the ground.

Fortunately for me, my neighbor Diane Vilas was working in her yard and saw what happened. At first she thought that I had hurt my leg, but when she saw my legs and arm twitching, she knew time was of the essence.

Next door to Diane lived her stepdaughter, Susan. Susan was a nurse, and she immediately called EMS. By the time they put me in the ambulance, the entire left side of my body was paralyzed. Apparently I had a clot on the right side of my brain that had stopped the flow of blood and oxygen to the left side of my body.

When I reached Our Lady of the Lake Hospital, it had only been a few minutes since I collapsed. Cardiologist Carl Luikart, neurologist Jay Acosta, and a team of physicians and nurses immediately began working on me. Acosta told Helen that there was a shot called TPA that they could give me to prevent permanent paralysis but that it may cause internal bleeding. He explained that there was a 96 percent chance that I would be fine, but there still remained a 4 percent chance of cerebral bleeding and possibly death.

Helen was never one to gamble but liked the odds. For her own peace of mind, she asked the doctor what he would do if it were one of his loved ones. He said to try the shot.

The medical staff was working against the clock, as the shot had to be injected within three hours of the stroke happening. Otherwise, irreversible paralysis would set in. The stroke happened at 9:30 AM, and the shot was finally administered at 10:55. Part of the fluid was rapidly injected into my body, and the rest was allowed to slowly enter my system via intravenous drip. At 11:55 all of the fluid was inside me. The doctors and nurses had won the battle against the clock, but only time would tell if their efforts had paid off.

Within an hour or two, I was moving my arms, legs, and eyes and talking clearly. I am so blessed to have had such a spectacular team of doctors attending to me. Helen said it was like witnessing a miracle!

I ended up spending three days in intensive care and five days in cardiac care. My heart was out of rhythm, and the doctors felt that was the reason for the stroke in the first place

Nothing had ever hit me like that. I've been banged around and suffered light concussions here and there but recovered immediately. This time, the lights just went out. It was terrifying. I realize how blessed I am, and I wake up every morning thanking the Good Lord he had reason to keep me here.

Chapter  46

In Retrospect

I was just a player. I enjoyed football. I enjoyed contact. I guess it's unusual, knowing that you're going to have some pain and have some suffering, and looking forward to it. And have a very strong, positive attitude. You're focused on your position and your job, and once they give you that football—hand off to you—you're focused on picking up yards for the Green Bay Packers football team.

I just tried to be the best possible football player I could be down in and down out. Maybe some players don't have the same attitude. Winning is part of the reward, but there's no guarantee that you are going to win, that you are going to be a Pro Bowler. There's none of that going to happen for sure.

People evaluate on a scale. After you work hard and you accomplish something—maybe win two or three games—then you lose two or three, and you're right between a rock and a hard place. You have to ask yourself why are you losing? Why can't you overcome that? Why can't you beat down and work harder and focus more?

Everybody can't win. I accept that. There are going to be half-winners and half-losers. But still there's something inside, something you determine by choice—whether you're a winner or a loser. If you accept being a loser, that's what you're going to be. It's that thing inside of you that can make you a winner. It's not your legs that gain the yards.

Everybody has size, everybody has speed, and everybody has strength. There were another 1,000 or 10,000 football players who had the same opportunities I did. They all had average ability. They all had legs and arms and a heart, but they still did not produce as I did.

And that was by choice.

Chapter

Giving Back

A New Beginning

With my company dissolved and a new marriage to Helen, I had a lot of free time. My mother always told my brothers and me to never forget where we came from and to always give back. Many former NFL players have now become motivational speakers. This was never my forté, but I always enjoyed participating in charity golf tournaments while representing the Saints.

After my induction into the Pro Football Hall of Fame in 1976, I guess I became somewhat of a celebrity, because all of a sudden I began receiving invitations to hundreds of charity golf classics all over the nation. Because I finally had the time to do so, I decided that I would help raise money for the needy and at the same time, play a little golf.

For the past 40-plus years, I have played in literally hundreds of celebrity/charity golf events all over the country. I would like to share with you some of my experiences with charitable organizations.

The Bing Crosby National Pro Amateur Golf Championship was originated by Bing in 1937 at Rancho Santa Fe Golf Club. In 1947 the event moved to Pebble Beach.

The reason behind the pro-am was to raise money for charity. But as the charity continued throughout the years, it turned out that the pro golfers were receiving more money than the charity. This was not Bing's intent.

Crosby died in 1977 and his widow, Kathryn, moved the tournament to the Bermuda Run Country Club in North Carolina. She also changed the format of the event to a celebrity tournament, where she didn't have to pay the pro golfers. It turned out to be the kind of charity contest that Bing would have been proud of.

Each year more than 200 celebrities from the fields of entertainment, sports, politics, etc. come together for a week to raise millions of dollars for the various charities. I participated in the Crosby Open for 15 years.

Whomever won the Crosby had the opportunity to choose the charity or charities to which they wanted their winnings to be donated. All of my winnings went to Johnny Robinson's Boys Home, local food banks, and cancer centers. It makes me feel good to know that in some small way, I have made someone's life a little better.

The Frank Sinatra Celebrity Invitational was started by Sinatra in 1988 and has assisted more than 100,000 children at the Barbara Sinatra Children's Center at Eisenhower Medical Center in Palm Springs. I played in this tournament for many years and donated various auction items to help raise money for the center. It is extremely heartwarming to know that I have helped a child.

In 1971, one year after Coach Lombardi's death, the Vince Lombardi Golf Classic was created and became a fund-raiser for the Cancer Hospital in Milwaukee, Wisconsin. Bart and Cherry Starr are the cohosts for the event. I have many wonderful memories of this tournament because it honors the man I loved so very much. Over the years it has raised thousands of dollars for cancer research.

Prior to the tournament, Helen and I would always participate in the Lombardi Run to Daylight run. It was a 5K race that loosened me up a bit for my golf game!

My best memory of that tournament is from 1983. My teammates and I started off on the back nine in the early morning tee-off. Upon completing the back nine, we stopped for lunch, then continued on to the front nine.

On hole number two was parked a brand new 1983 Buick Century. It was just sitting there waiting for someone to make a hole in one.

It was a par 3 and about 170 yards to the hole. My other teammates chose their clubs and teed off. It was then my turn to address the ball. I moved up to my position and took a practice swing. I set up on the ball and smacked it high into the air. It came down and bounced high into the air. At the hole where the pin was placed stood quite a few spectators. The ball rolled and rolled then disappeared. Everyone began to yell and applaud. I wasn't sure what had happened, so we got into our carts and went to find my ball.

As we arrived at the upper level, the fans were shouting, "It's a hole in one!" There was my new car, just sitting there waiting for me to take it home!

It was my first and only hole in one! What a day! This tournament only takes place a few days in June, but it has helped so many people over the years.

My Tournament

The Mary Bird Perkins Cancer Center Golf Classic began in Baton Rouge in 1990. In 1992 I added my name to the tournament billing, and Helen and I hosted the event. Between 1990 and 1991 alone, I had received more than 200 golf and tennis charity invitations. It was time for me to organize and plan one at home.

I called upon many of my celebrity friends to help me out. We had 35 people commit from the NFL and Baseball Hall of Fame, along with motion picture actors and comedians.

In 1991 the tournament netted $39,000. Helen and I were determined and committed to set an all-time event record. We set up a committee of hardworking people. As with the key to any event of this nature, donations are critical. Northwest Airlines generously donated all of the airline tickets to all celebs who participated. The Hilton Hotels practically gave us the rooms for free and allowed us to use the Presidential Suite as our Hospitality Room and the Grand Ballroom for our award parties. World-renowned Louisiana chef John Folse helped us establish a Taste of Louisiana with 20 of our state's best chefs donating their signature dishes to the cause. The food was unbelievable as each chef tried his and her best to outdo the others.

Our Jack Nicklaus Course at the Country Club of Louisiana was then owned by Chuck McCoy, a Baton Rouge banker and philanthropist. For a very small fee, he allowed us to use the club and course. The donations for the silent and live auctions kept pouring in. The tournament turned out to be a huge success. We made more than $250,000. With that money, the Mary Bird Perkins Cancer Center bought a new state-of-the art piece of equipment that could detect malignant brain tumors.

The hard work and coordination of a timeline by volunteer workers orchestrating my charity golf tournament gave me a new appreciation for all the previous events I had attended.

Other Charity Classics

One golf charity classic that I participated in will live in my heart forever.

For many years, professional golfer Andy North and the Rayovac company hosted a golf tournament at Maple Bluff Country Club in Madison, Wisconsin, for the Special Olympics. During one of the associated awards dinners, the Special Olympics participants came into the room and took pictures with the celebrities. They also thanked us for supporting them.

One of the celebrities, Olympic speed skater Dan Jansen from Wisconsin, stood up to speak. I will never forget the story he told. It was extremely moving.

Dan had just finished competing in the 1988 Winter Olympics. He had been favored to win both the 500- and 1,000-meter races. However, in the early morning hours of the day of the race, he received a phone call saying that his sister Jane was dying of leukemia. Later that morning she died.

With the commitment that he had made to his country to compete, Dan began his 500-meter race but took a bad fall early on in the competition. A few days later he competed in the 1,000-meter race only to repeat what had happened in the 500. He left the 1988 Olympics without winning any medals. All of his dreams and hard work seemed to have gone up in smoke. He was totally devastated. Thousands of compassionate letters came to him from all over the world. They explained to Dan how sorry they were to hear of his sister's death and encouraged him to compete in the next Winter Olympics in 1992.

One of the most touching letters came from a Special Olympian. He sent Dan his gold medal and said, "I know how hard I worked for this. I want you to have it."

Dan then promised the Special Olympian he would be back in four years and would win the gold for all Americans—especially the Special Olympians—and he did just that!

There wasn't a dry eye in the room.

Another charity that I am proud to have played in for many years is the Mickey Mantle Golf Classic in Las Vegas and his other tournament in Tulsa, Oklahoma. Mickey's charity was the children's Make-A-Wish Foundation.

At one of Mickey's live auctions, there was a 1932 baby-blue Plymouth convertible up for grabs. The minimum bid was $17,000. Mickey leaned over to me from his table and told me that the first car he ever owned was a 1932 baby-blue Plymouth, but it was a hardtop not a convertible. He also said that he would really like to have it.

Mantle bid $17,000 on the car and won it. The following year, he donated it back to the Make-A-Wish Foundation. That's the kind of guy he was.

In 1980 I played in the United States Blind Golfers Association Pro Am Classic at the New Orleans Country Club. There I met a blind golfer named Pat Brown.

In 1966 Pat was in a car accident that severed his optic nerve. He immediately lost his vision. After a long hospital recovery, he was able to go back and practice law. A few years later he found out that there was a National Blind Golfers Association. His son Patrick III taught his father that he didn't need his vision to continue playing golf.

Pat played in his first tournament in 1969 and won his first national title in 1975. He continued to win the national title for the next 20 years.

I feel so privileged to have met this man. What an inspiration.

Among the many, many other charities I have participated in over the years are:

- The Nabisco/Dinah Shore Tournament and Bob Hope Classic—multiple charities
- Perry Como's The Duke Classic (later hosted by Jeff Foxworthy)—a fundraiser for Children's Hospital at Duke University
- Bobby Mitchell Hall of Fame Golf Classic—a fundraiser for leukemia
- Chuck Bednarik's Good Shepherd Classic—a fundraiser for the Good Shepherd Hospital

- Marty Lyons' and Joe Namath's Golf Classics—for local charities
- Nick Buoniconti's the Cure for Paralysis—for research
- Deacon Jones' the Deacon Jones Foundation—for local charities
- Ray Nitschke Annual Golf Classic—for local charities
- Jan Stenerud—for the Special Olympics
- Bert Jones—for Cystic Fibrosis
- Roger Maris Golf Classic (hosted by Bob Costas)—for local charities
- Jim Palmer's Golf Classic—for Cystic Fibrosis
- Don Drysdale's Hall of Fame Classic—for local charities
- The Ben, Willie, and Darrell Classic (Ben Crenshaw, Willie Nelson, and Darrell Royal)—for at-risk youth in Austin, Texas
- Patricia Neal's Golf Classic—for the physically handicapped
- Sam Walton's Golf Classic—for cancer research
- Marlo Thomas and Phil Donahue Golf Tournament—for St. Jude's
- Every Super Bowl Classic since its creation—Caring for Kids programs
- Pro Bowl Tournaments—Caring for Kids programs
- Nick Nicolosi and the NFL Golf and Bowling Tournaments (for 25 years)—Caring for Kids programs
- The Jim Thorpe Classic (being a former Jim Thorpe winner myself)—for local charities
- The Heisman Trophy Classic—for local charities
- LSU Tiger Athletic Foundation and Alumni Golf Events—for scholarships
- Baton Rouge High School Golf Tournament—for school computers and supplies
- Louisiana Sports Hall of Fame Golf Classic—for the Shriners Hospitals for Children
- Pro Football Hall of Fame Golf Classic—for Enshrinees Assistance Fund

I have also participated in many of the Celebrity Pro Am Tennis Classics with tennis greats Rod Laver, Chris Evert, and Pancho Gonzales. One time I was even paired up with Rene Richards!

The NFL Snoring Contest

In 2003 Breathe Right partnered with the Pro Football Hall of Fame to launch the "Search for the NFL's Loudest Snorer of All Time."

Helen decided she would enter me in this contest. She sent the judges a 50-word jingle stating why I should be crowned the loudest snorer in the NFL. At that time, Ahman Green with the Packers had just broken one of my longstanding Packers rushing records. Helen took this into consideration and wrote her jingle. Here's how it went:

I snore so loud I could wake the dead.

Sure enough, Coach Lombardi appeared.

I told him somebody needed to invent strips to make it easier to breathe on icy Lambeau Field.

With a box of Breathe Right Strips, I can return and beat Ahman Green's record!

In January 2004 we received a letter stating that Helen's jingle was the NFC winner. We won $7,500 in spending money, two airline tickets to Houston for the Super Bowl, and six nights at the Four Seasons. I was to compete against AFC winner Bobby Bell. The winner would get $10,000 donated to his favorite charity and the runner-up would get $5,000 donated to his favorite charity.

Helen recorded my snoring so it could be played at the event. She sent it to Breathe Right.

On the Tuesday before the Super Bowl, Bobby Bell and I were at the Brown Convention Center in Houston for the competition. On stage there were two beds—one with my name on it and one with Bobby's name on it. In the middle of the two beds was a Snore-O-Meter, which registered the decibels of the snoring.

Former 49ers great Jerry Rice was the emcee that evening. He introduced both Bobby and me, and a panel of judges listened to both of our recorded snoring examples. Bobby scored high, but when it was my turn, the decibels from the Snore-O-Meter went off the chart!

Jerry Rice came over and placed the coveted Breathe Right Nightcap on my head and announced me as the NFL's Loudest Snorer.

A check for $10,000 was presented to me for our charity, the Food Bank of Baton Rouge. I also received a year's supply of Breathe Right Strips.

It was a lot of fun and for a very worthy cause.

The Loyal Fans of Green Bay

Even though I haven't suited up in more than 40 years, I still continue to receive letters from football fans. I can't tell you how much I appreciate these folks taking the time to write to me. It is very heartwarming to know that the game I loved so much meant so much to so many.

When I was playing for Green Bay, I was very close to the fans, and to this day I have kept in touch with many of them. A camaraderie of this type is special, and I feel extremely fortunate to have it.

One day a few years ago I received a phone call from Mickie, the daughter of Vernon Thome, a car dealer in Green Bay and a Packers fanatic. She told me that Ray Nitschke had given her my phone number. Her father, Vernon, had been diagnosed with terminal brain cancer.

I had known Vernon for many years. He had a used-car lot in Green Bay. I lived in Green Bay during the season, and each year I would buy a used car from him. I'd even go out to his lot and help him wash the cars!

Vernon had bought his two sons, Greg and Chip, a set of weights. I would go over to their home and show the boys how to use them.

Mickie asked if I wouldn't mind speaking to her dad to cheer him up a little. She told me that on her father's bedroom wall was an autographed photo of Coach Lombardi and me. It was one of her dad's most prized possessions.

Well, Vernon got on the phone and we began reminiscing about some of the great times we used to have. We spoke for quite a while.

When Mickie got back on the phone, she told me that that was the first time she had seen her dad smile and laugh in weeks. She thanked me. From that day forward, I called and checked on my Green Bay buddy on a daily basis.

Three weeks later, Ray Nitschke suffered an unexpected heart attack and died. Helen and I were flying to Green Bay for the funeral. While waiting to change planes in Chicago, I called Mickie and asked if we could visit her dad that evening. I told her that we would be landing in Green Bay about 5:00, picking up a rental car, and going to check into our hotel.

All of a sudden, Mickie began to cry. She couldn't believe that I was coming out to see her dad. She told me to cancel my rental car, and that she would pick us up, bring us to the house to see her dad, then drop us off at the hotel.

Upon arriving at Vernon's home, I had really only intended to stay about 15 minutes or so. I knew how very sick and weak he was. But we began telling stories and laughing so much that the 15 minutes turned into two hours! It was such a special visit.

The following day, Vernon's son drove us to Ray's funeral and then on to the airport. A few weeks later, Vernon passed away.

His children called and thanked me for coming over to see their dad. They said that my visit meant a lot to him. I told them that it also meant a lot to me.

The following Christmas Helen and I received a card from Mickie saying what a wonderful relationship Lombardi and our team had with the town of Green Bay. She also told us about the Green Bay players of today and how they are not that involved with the people and fans of the city.

How sad that is. I will always cherish the fans who supported us. They were the greatest fans in the league!

Chapter 49

I've Truly Been Blessed

When I think about my family and friends, I realize how truly blessed I have been.

My children have grown up in the New Orleans area and have stayed close by over the years. My daughter JoBeth is married, and she and her husband Mike have two beautiful daughters, Melissa (Missy) and Jessica. Missy, our oldest granddaughter, has graduated from the University of New Orleans with a degree in finance and is married with two sons, Emilio and Jose. My son Chip is married, and he and his wife Sherry have our only grandson, James Taylor III, and two beautiful daughters, Lauren and Erin.

My brothers Clark and Webb both still live in Baton Rouge close to Helen and me. Clark, the attorney and real-estate developer, still goes to the office a few days a week. He loves to fish and stays very active playing tennis at Bocage Racquet Club. Webb, my younger brother, has retired from accounting and enjoys his time on the golf course. He is the best golfer in our family and has traveled with me to many of the charity golf classics.

My wonderful wife, Helen, has one sister, Georgi, who we are very close to. She is married to Clark Irwin and lives in Springdale, Arkansas. Their two girls, Carrie and Lauren, have both graduated from college and are married and living in Texas. We have made many family trips together over the years. We went on a cruise to Alaska and later visited Lauren when she was living in Madrid, Spain, studying Spanish while at SMU. Clark and his brother Jim played football at Arkansas under Lou Holtz, so it is always fun when LSU plays Arkansas!

My mother's youngest brother, Uncle Nathan Brown, died in 2008 and we lost Helen's mom, Sara, in 2009. They were both in their 90s and had full lives, but we miss them both. We are now the older generation, and as the saying goes: "As in golf, if you are over 50, you're on the back nine. You just don't know what hole you are on!"

With both Helen and I growing up in Baton Rouge, we have stayed friends with many of our junior high, high school, and LSU classmates. We are members of the Broadmoor United Methodist Church in Baton Rouge and are very active with Sunday school classes. We participate in our food-bank drive and Habitat for Humanity. We have an unbelievable support group of friends from our church and community.

God has always been No. 1 in my life. My faith has allowed me to get through the good and bad times. I have been truly blessed!

Vignettes, Write-Ups, and Stats

The Taylor Torture

By Bill Curry, former Green Bay Packers teammate
August 28, 2005

Jimmy Taylor had stood out on my visit to the Green Bay locker room in Dallas. He had stood out in heroic fashion in the 1962 NFL Championship Game against the New York Giants. He had stood out any time he had taken on tacklers as if they were tenpins in a bowling alley. There was more to come.

Somehow my locker was placed next to Jimmy, who was dubbed "Doodle Bird" by Tommy Joe Crutcher, the Will Rogers of our team. As bad as his nickname was, it was better than the one Hornung had hung on me.

Taylor fascinated me so much I had a hard time resisting the urge to stare. It was fun to watch and listen as he glanced around the room and issued quips under his breath.

"Look at Nitschke. Ain't he a trip? Huh? Look, Henry [Jordan] has got Robbie [Dave Robinson] all hot and bothered again. Wow, huh? Do you think Bigboy Marshall can make our team? He's missing a finger, you know that."

About halfway through training camp he turned to me and asked, "You lifted a little, haven't you, kid?"

I answered that I had and that I was beginning to wish I had lifted more.

"Good," he said. "You and I are going to do some bench presses today."

"What?" I gulped. "We're in two-a-days, Mr. Taylor. Nobody lifts weights during two-a-days."

He said, "I do, and pretty soon you will too, kid."

"Well, I don't think so, Mr. Taylor. I need all the energy I have just to make it through the day," I implored him.

"Nah, you can do it. Just come with me when I tell you," he insisted.

Orders from future Hall of Fame fullbacks are rare, and I assure you they have an impact on the delicate psyches of rookies.

That afternoon I tried my best to avoid Taylor. I quickly wrapped my ankles, went by the equipment room, put on my pads, and sneaked over to visit friends in the defensive room, which was separate from ours. I heard him coming.

He hollered, "Hey, kid, let's go! Get your pads off and follow me!" as he strode through the defensive room on his way to the tiny weight room.

He was dressed only in a jock and a cutoff T-shirt, his bulging muscles and washboard abs prominent. He grinned that same little grin I had seen in Dallas.

"Thought you could escape, huh, kid?" He chuckled. "Come on with me, you'll be glad you did."

We both knew that his interest was more in having a spotter for bench-pressing than in a last-round pick becoming stronger, but there was no way out. Not long after we had begun, I spotted Coach Lombardi passing by. I figured at least that I would earn a few points with our coach for the extra work, so I grunted and pushed with all my might. He scowled and faced us. "Don't strain!" he barked. "Wonderful!"

Lombardi's two-a-day regimen was different than any other I had encountered. The morning practices were conducted in shorts and T-shirts. We didn't wear headgear—something I thought was terribly risky. Practice began with an incredible series of calisthenics and grass drills. Assistant coach Tom Fears led them, and they were gut-checks from the very beginning.

They seemed as though they had lasted for an eternity and were followed by the dreaded up-downs known as grass drills. They were called up-downs because one runs in place until the leader blows a whistle. It was here that Lombardi always took over. On the whistle, we were all to dive forward onto the ground. At the second blast, we were to jump up, commence running in place again, and so on. Ken Bowman and I kept count, and there were days we got into the 70s on reps. I think the record was 78.

By about rep number 40, guys were heaving their breakfast, stumbling glassy-eyed, staying on one knee, or being carted off by the trainers. On and on the whistle sounded, followed by Lombardi's admonitions: "Get up! Damnit, get up! Fatigue makes cowards of us all! Get up!!"

For me it became surreal as I watched in wonder as my superheroes flagged in their efforts to stay with the sadistic whistle. Bowman was the starting center, and he and I took great pride in the fact that we performed every single rep. We didn't look very good doing it, but somehow we pushed through the fatigue. Most everyone else took breaks, vomited, or slowed up.

But not Jimmy Taylor. Taylor leapt to his feet, drove his huge thighs and knees upward like a prancing pony, dove out, caught himself palms flat, and exploded into the next rep with his mighty arms. He kept his head and shoulders erect, his flat-top head straight ahead, and though I could never see his face, I imagined that little smirk of a smile on it throughout the torture. It was amazing, and it drove Coach Lombardi into ecstasy every day.

"Jimmy Taylor! Way to go, Jimmy! Watch Taylor work! Atta boy, Jimmy! By God, Jimmy Taylor knows how to get in shape!" he shouted with even more than the normal volume.

Bowman and I drove ourselves, hoping to be noticed and to get into the Taylor school of high praise with Coach, but it never happened.

After the final grass drill, which was entirely a function of Coach Lombardi's mood and judgment of our team conditioning, he blew the whistle in a loud, long blast. That was the signal to take off as a team, around the goalpost at the south end of the field, then a left turn and a sprint to the agility area at the east side of the adjacent field, a run of roughly 200 yards. It seemed like miles, and except for the gazelles like

Taylor and receivers Bob Long and Carroll Dale, it was another murderous combination of heaving chests, retching guts, and wobbly knees.

When we reached our destination, Lombardi would begin shouting, "Don't be last!"

God help you if you were last. We could never catch the receivers or Taylor, but Bowman and I were among the first linemen to the team area every day. We stood and watched the big guys drag their massive bodies through the last 30 or 40 yards, often falling across the imaginary line to cries from Lombardi of "Get up! Get up, damnit! You cannot play football on the ground!"

Finally there was a respite. The sound of the heavy breathing from 80 or 90 team candidates is one of those riveting memories that will never leave me. It was something like a herd of thoroughbreds on a horse farm, having done their morning run in a group, gathering at the water trough. Here were huge, fast, well-functioning systems that normal mortals could never comprehend, breathing in unison, almost in concert, as if there were a conductor's baton counting the cadence. My guess is that this was one of Coach Lombardi's favorite moments.

He called us up, told us to take a knee, and then surveyed the wreckage. After all these years it occurred to me for the first time that these moments constituted another of Lombardi's many areas of genius. He could read his team at moments of extreme stress. He watched, badgered, pushed, and cajoled us, and learned who would and who would not push through the pain. He observed, made team cuts in his mind, and addressed the troops. Obviously he was better at reading the signals than his rival coaches.

In my two years with the team he spent very little time talking in these hyperventilated moments, but he delivered crucial pronouncements on team and individual conditioning that meant a great deal to us. Not only did they affect the waiver wire, but they had a bearing on the duration of future grass drills.

When I reported for my second year, Jimmy Taylor took me aside after the first day and said, "Look here, kid; you are a veteran now, huh?" He spoke softly with a clipped staccato delivery.

"Yeah, Jimmy, I am a veteran," I responded.

I had not progressed with him to Doodle Bird, but we had gotten past Mr. Taylor.

"Ya gotta be a leader now, right, huh? Ya know what I mean?"

He eyeballed me.

"I do, and I agree," I answered, happy to be having a peer conversation.

"OK," he continued. "You've got some improving to do, got that kid?"

Improving! What the hell? I was expecting compliments for doing every grass drill and being one of the first linemen around the goalposts.

"Yeah, kid, you need to do one thing better. You're pretty good on the up-downs and you make the run okay, but when we gather up, you gotta do better. The rookies will be watching."

I was angry now and shot back, "Do better at the team meeting? Great, I'll work on it tomorrow."

"Aw, come on, kid, don't get pissed with me for trying to make you into a real leader. Just *listen*."

"OK, what can I do to please you?" I said, realizing I couldn't help but be impressed by his sincerity.

What followed blew me away and forever became part of my makeup as a player and as a coach. Jimmy Taylor looked me squarely in the eye and said in utter seriousness, "When we finish our run around the goalposts, don't breathe so hard."

Don't breathe so hard?

I looked for a hint of a smile in his eyes and found none.

"Yeah," he said. "You can't breathe so hard and be a good leader...makes you look tired. Don't ever let anybody know you're tired. Don't ever let Lombardi know he's killing you. Don't concede anything to anybody."

I asked, "And just how does a man do all that work and not breathe hard? You are asking the impossible."

Wrong response to Jimmy Taylor. He raised his voice and said, "Impossible? Nothing is impossible, kid! How bad you want to be a leader? Damnit, don't you tell me something is impossible. You can do it, kid! I tell you what, just watch me tomorrow. I will come around that last curve, run the straightaway like a rocket, pull up, stretch my hamstrings, smile, and just blow it out."

I said, "What do you mean, blow it out?"

"Just watch me, kid. I go *phew* one time, and that's it. Then I just stand there like nothing has happened. Watch me, kid."

I did, and as I live and breathe (no pun), he did it!

As surely as Willie Davis had changed the way I saw other people, Jimmy Taylor changed the way I regarded conditioning, the way I wanted teammates and coaches to perceive me, and just as important, the way I wanted opponents to see me.

"Don't concede anything to anybody" became my mantra for survival in the National Football League, in coaching, and in life. It was one more example of a great player offering an unexpected, undeserved, unrewarded act of kindness to an impressionable youngster.

What I believe is that we should respect everyone. Concede nothing. Thanks, Jimmy Taylor, and God bless you.

Taylor's All-Time Statistics

Jim Taylor became the Packers' bread-and-butter guy. Vince Lombardi depended on him to get the needed short yardage, whether it was for a first down or a touchdown.

As the Packers dynasty grew, so, too, did Taylor become the symbol of power in the awesome Green Bay attack. Jim was a throwback to an earlier era, who ran with a fierceness no one could match. He caught the short swing passes and blocked with rugged determination.

Thousand-yard seasons became a specialty for Taylor. He went over 1,000 yards five straight seasons beginning in 1960 but reached his zenith in 1962, when he had a career-high 1,474 yards and was named the NFL Player of the Year.

Jim was living testimony to the popular football adage, "When the going gets tough, the tough get going." Nowhere was this more evident than in the 1962 NFL title game. Playing on a bitterly cold day, Taylor engaged in a personal duel with the New York Giants' outstanding defense led by All-Pro linebacker Sam Huff. Jim carried 31 times for 85 yards and scored Green Bay's only touchdown in a 16–7 victory. He took a fearful pounding both from the hard-hitting Giants and the frozen ground. He suffered an elbow gash that took seven stitches to close at halftime and a badly cut tongue. At the end, he could barely see, and he couldn't talk.

Taylor was often compared with Jim Brown, the Cleveland Browns' fullback, who played at the same time. There were many different viewpoints, but Lombard'is summation was most succinct: "Jim Brown will give you that leg and then take it away from you. Jim Taylor will give it to you and then ram it through your chest!"

Year	Team	G	No.	Yds.	Avg.	D	No.	Yds.	Avg.	TD
1958	Green Bay	12	52	247	4.8	1	4	72	18.0	1
1959	Green Bay	12	120	452	3.8	6	9	71	7.9	2
1960	Green Bay	12	230	1101	4.8	11	15	121	8.1	0
1961	Green Bay	14	243	1307	5.4	15	25	175	7.0	1
1962	Green Bay	14	272	1474	5.4	19	22	106	4.8	0
1963	Green Bay	14	248	1018	4.1	9	13	68	5.2	1
1964	Green Bay	13	235	1169	5.0	12	38	354	9.3	3
1965	Green Bay	13	207	734	3.5	4	20	207	10.4	0
1966	Green Bay	14	204	705	3.5	4	41	331	8.1	2
1967	New Orleans	14	130	390	3.0	2	38	251	6.6	0
Career Total		**132**	**1941**	**8597**	**4.4**	**83**	**225**	**1756**	**7.8**	**10**

Additional Career Statistics: Kickoff Returns: 7-185

Reference: Pro Football Hall of Fame

Season Records and Team Standings

YEAR	TEAM	SEASON RECORD	DIVISION FINISH
1958	Green Bay Packers	1–10–1	6th Place
1959	Green Bay Packers	7–5–0	Tied for 3rd Place
1960	Green Bay Packers	8–4–0	1st Place
1961	Green Bay Packers	11–3–0	1st Place
1962	Green Bay Packers	13–1–0	1st Place
1963	Green Bay Packers	11–2–1	2nd Place
1964	Green Bay Packers	8–5–1	Tied for 2nd Place
1965	Green Bay Packers	10–3–1	Tied for 1st Place
1966	Green Bay Packers	12–2–0	1st Place
1967	New Orleans Saints	3–11–0	4th Place

10 playing seasons—132 games

Championship Games
1960—Philadelphia 17, Green Bay 13
Taylor starting fullback for Green Bay. Along with Bart Starr, led the march that gave the Packers a 13–10 lead late in the game. Reached 9-yard line of Eagles on pass reception as game ended. Rushed 24 times for 105 yards. Caught six passes for 46 yards.

1961—Green Bay 37, New York 0
Rushed 14 times for 69 yards, including one 33-yarder, longest rush of game.

1962—Green Bay 16, New York 7
Starting fullback for Green Bay. This game involved his famous "duel" with New York linebacker Sam Huff. Taylor carried record 31 times for 85 yards. Also caught three passes for 20 yards. Scored Green Bay's only TD on seven-yard run.

1965 Divisional Playoff—Green Bay 13, Baltimore 10 (Overtime)
Starting fullback for Green Bay. Again a workhorse with 23 carries for 60 yards and two receptions for 29 yards.

1965—Green Bay 23, Cleveland 12
Carried 27 times for 96 yards and caught two passes for 20 yards.

1966—Green Bay 34, Dallas 27
Starting fullback for Green Bay. Carried 10 times for 37 yards and caught five passes for 23 yards.

Championship Records—NFC (at time of retirement)
Most rushes, lifetime—106

Most rushes, game—31 vs. New York in 1962, tied with Steve Van Buren in 1949; and 27 vs. Cleveland in 1965, tied for third

Most yards rushing, lifetime—392

Most combined attempts, lifetime—122

Most combined attempts, game—34 vs. New York in 1962 and 30 vs. Philadelphia in 1960 (third)

Most combined yardage, lifetime—501

Super Bowl Record
Super Bowl I—Green Bay 35, Kansas City 10
Starting fullback for Green Bay. Scored go-ahead touchdown on 14-yard run in second quarter. Game's leading rusher with 56 yards on 17 rushes. Caught one pass for minus-one-yard loss.

All-League Teams
1962—AP, UPI

Statistical Highlights
Led NFL in rushing in 1962 with 1,474 yards
Led NFL in scoring in 1962 with 114 points
Led NFL in rushing TDs in 1961 with 15 and in 1962 with 19
No. 3 all-time NFL rusher with 8,597 yards

In the Record Book—NFL Regular Season (at time of retirement)
Most rushing attempts, lifetime—1,941 (second behind Jim Brown)
Most yards rushing, lifetime—8,597 (second behind Jim Brown)
Most games, 100 yards or more rushing—26 (third behind Jim Brown and Leroy Kelly)
Most games, 100 yards or more rushing in a season—7 (tied for third)
Most touchdowns rushing, lifetime—83 (second behind Jim Brown)
Most touchdowns rushing, season—19 (1962)
Most combined attempts, lifetime—2,180 (second behind Jim Brown)

Pro Bowls
Selected to four Pro Bowls—1961, 1962, 1963 (did not play), and 1964

Pro Bowl Highlights
1961—Starting fullback for West. Scored three TDs as West won 35–31. Touchdowns came on plunges of two, one, and three yards.
1962—Starting fullback for West, which won 31–30. Taylor didn't score but was leading West rusher with 27 yards on seven carries. Also had one pass reception for six yards.

1964—Starting fullback for West, which won 31–17. Taylor scored the first West touchdown on a 37-yard run. He carried 14 times for 98 yards and also caught one pass for one yard.

1965—Starting fullback for West, which won 34–14. Carried 10 times for 28 yards and caught two passes for eight yards.

The All-Lombardi Team

By Chuck Johnson of the *Milwaukee Journal* (1968)

Offense:
Flanker—Max McGee (1959–1967)
Split End—Boyd Dowler (1959–1967)
Tight End—Ron Kramer (1959–1964)
Left Tackle—Bob Skoronski (1959–1967)
Left Guard—Fred "Fuzzy" Thurston (1959–1967)
Center—Jim Ringo (1959–1963)
Right Guard—Jerry Kramer (1959–1967)
Right Tackle—Forrest Gregg (1959–1967)
Quarterback—Bart Starr (1959–1967)
Fullback—Jim Taylor (1959–1966)
Halfback—Paul Hornung (1959–1962, 1964–1966)
Kicker—Don Chandler (1965–1967)

Defense:

Left End—Willie Davis (1960–1967)

Left Tackle—Ron Kostelnik (1961–1967)

Right Tackle—Henry Jordan (1959–1967)

Right End—Lionel Aldridge (1963–1967)

Left Linebacker—Dave Robinson (1963–1967)

Middle Linebacker—Ray Nitschke (1959–1967)

Right Linebacker—Lee Roy Caffey (1964–1967)

Left Halfback—Herb Adderley (1961–1967)

Right Halfback—Bob Jeter (1963–1967)

Left Safety—Tom Brown (1964–1967)

Right Safety—Willie Wood (1960–1967)

The Green Bay Draft: The Taylor Years (1958–1966)

1958: In 1958 assistant coach Ray "Scooter" McLean succeeded Lisle Blackbourn as the new Packers coach. Ray had become an assistant coach with Green Bay watching the Packers struggle with a 3–9 mark in 1951 under the leadership of coach Gene Ronzani. At the beginning of the 1958 Packers season an air of optimism seemed to blanket the team. Prior to our first game, Coach McLean told the *Green Bay Press-Gazette*, "We're not shooting for just a good season; we're going after the championship." That line of thinking quickly changed to resentment and despair as we lost the first game, tied the second, and then continued to lose nine of our last 10 games. Our 1–10–1 record was the worst in the history of the franchise.

1958 Draft Class
Dan Currie—LB—Michigan State
Jim Taylor—FB—LSU*
Dick Christy—HB—North Carolina State

*Indicates Hall of Fame member

Ray Nitschke—LB—Illinois*
Jerry Kramer—G—Idaho
Ken Gray—G—Howard Payne
Gene Cook—E—Toledo

1959: Our first Packers team under the tutelage of Coach Lombardi didn't take long to better the dismal 1–10–1 record of the 1958 squad. Our 1959 team won its first three games and astounded the rest of the league. We lost our next five games—which turned out to be the longest losing streak in the Lombardi era—but three of the losses were to the then–division champion Baltimore Colts and New York Giants. We finished the regular season with four straight victories over the Redskins, Lions, Rams, and 49ers to post a final 7–5 record, the first .500-plus finish for Green Bay in 12 years. Lombardi had convinced us that we could win.

1959 Draft Class
Randy Duncan—QB—Iowa
Alex Hawkins—HB—South Carolina
Boyd Dowler—FL—Colorado
Andy Cvercko—G—Northwestern
Bobby G. Jackson—DB—Alabama
Bob Laraba—LB—Texas-Western
Bill Butler—DB—Tennessee-Chattanooga
Dave Smith—FB—Ripon
Joe Hergert—LB—Florida
Timmy Brown—RB—Ball State

1960: This was to be the Packers' first championship year in the Lombardi era. Green Bay was at the top of the Western Conference with an 8–4 record, finishing with three straight victories over the Chicago Bears, the San Francisco 49ers, and the Los Angeles Rams while the defending champion Baltimore Colts ended their season at 6–6. At first it had appeared that the Packers would be out of the race. In a short span of only five days we had lost to the Rams and Lions, giving us a 5–4 record. Our scouting director Jack Vainisi died and on the following Sunday we annihilated the Bears in Vainisi's hometown, Chicago, by a score of 41–13. We then thrashed the 49ers in a mud battle and clinched the title in Los Angeles. We lost our bid to the Eagles 17–13 in Philadelphia in the title battle but were deep in Eagles territory when the game ended.

1960 Draft Class

Tom Moore—HB—Vanderbilt

Bob Jeter—DB—Iowa

Dale Hackbart—DB—Wisconsin

Paul Winslow—DB—North Carolina Central

Jon Gilliam—C—Texas A&M Commerce

1961: In 1961 the league added two more teams to the schedule—Dallas and Minnesota. Just barely missing the league championship in 1960, the Packers were after the title with a vengeance. Unfortunately we lost our opener 17–13 to the Lions but ended up winning 10 of our next 11 games, losing only to the Colts in the eighth game before beating the Giants 20–17 to clinch the Western Conference title in the 12th game of the season. One of my personal highlights of the year was a 49–17 victory over the Cleveland Browns in Cleveland where I scored four touchdowns on runs of 25, 2, 45, and 4 yards. In the first title game ever held in Green Bay we shut out the New York Giants 37–0. In only three seasons, Lombardi had led the Packers from a previous 1–10–1 season to a 11–3–0 season and the world championship.

1961 Draft Class

Herb Adderley—DB—Michigan State*

Ron Kostelnik—DT—Cincinnati

Phil Nugent—DB—Tulane

Paul Dudley—HB—Arkansas

Lee Folkins—TE—Washington

Roger Hagberg—FB—Minnesota

Val Keckin—QB—Southern Miss

John Denvir—G—Colorado

Elijah Pitts—HB—Philander Smith

Nelson Toburen—LB—Wichita State

Jim Brewington—T—North Carolina Central

Ray Ratkowski—HB—Notre Dame

1962: Our 1961 Packers team is considered to be the best of the Lombardi era teams. This is based on our 13–1 regular-season record for a percentage of .929 and the world championship. We won our first 10 games, beating Baltimore twice before losing 26–14 to the Lions in Detroit. The Packers finished out the season with a two-game lead over Detroit and the title. At Yankee Stadium in freezing, blustering conditions, we once again beat the Giants for the NFL crown by a score of 16–7.

1962 Draft Class

Earl Gros—FB—LSU

Ed Blaine—G—Missouri

Gary Barnes—WR—Clemson

Ron Gassert—DT—Virginia

John Sutro—T—San Jose State

Oscar Donahue—WR—San Jose State

Gary Cutsinger—DE—Oklahoma State

Tom Pennington—K—Georgia

Ernie Green—HB—Louisville

1963: Even though the Packers ended the season with an 11–2–1 record, it wasn't good enough to win the Western Conference title. 1963 was the year of the Chicago Bears, who finished the season with an 11–1–2 record. As a matter of fact, two of Chicago's victories came at the expense of the Packers. Even still, it was a remarkable season as we played without Paul Hornung, who was suspended, and our quarterback Bart Starr, who was lost for half the season with injuries. The Packers made their first trip to the Playoff Bowl (which was held for the second-place teams of both the Western and Eastern Conferences) and beat the Cleveland Browns by a score of 40–23.

1963 Draft Class

Dave Robinson—LB—Penn State

Tom Brown—DB—Maryland

Dennis Claridge—QB—Nebraska

Tony Liscio—T—Tulsa

Lionel Aldridge—DE—Utah State

Dan Grimm—G—Colorado

Jan Barrett—E—Fresno State
Gary Kroner—DB—Wisconsin
Keith Kinderman—FB—Florida State
Marv Fleming—TE—Utah
Daryle Lamonica—QB—Notre Dame
Ed Holler—LB—South Carolina
Gene Breen—LB—Virginia Tech
Bobby Brezina—HB—Houston

1964: In 1964 a total of five points is all that was needed for us to lose three of our first six games. After a year's absence, Paul Hornung was unable to regain his kicking style. Missed extra points produced one-point losses to the Colts and Vikings and later in a must-win rematch at Baltimore. Paul missed five field goals in a 24–21 loss in the sixth game against the Colts, who finished the season with a strong 12–2–0 record. Finishing in second place once again, we gained a birth to the Playoff Bowl, but this time lost to the Cardinals 24–17.

1964 Draft Class

Lloyd Voss—DE—Nebraska
Jon Morris—C—Holy Cross
Ode Burrell—RB—Mississippi State
Joe O'Donnell—G—Michigan
Tommy Crutcher—LB—TCU
Bob Long—FL—Wichita State
Paul Costa—TE—Notre Dame
Steve Wright—T—Alabama
Ken Bowman—C—Wisconsin
John McDowell—T—St. John's (MN)
Allen Jacobs—FB—Utah
Len St. Jean—G—Northern Michigan
John W. Baker—DE—Norfolk State
Bill Curry—C—Georgia Tech

1965: Coach Lombardi referred to his 1965 Packers as "a team of character and dedication." It was a whirlwind, yet wonderful season. We won our first six games and then lost three of the next five. We ran all over the Colts in Baltimore 42–27 with five touchdowns by Hornung alone. A tie in the final game of the regular season forced the Colts and Green Bay into a sudden death Western Division playoff. We won in overtime on a Don Chandler field goal and then slammed the door on the Browns to once again regain the NFL championship.

1965 Draft Class

Donny Anderson—RB—Texas Tech

Larry Elkin—WR—Baylor

Al Dotson—DT—Grambling State

Allen Brown—TE—Mississippi

Jim Harvey—G—Mississippi

Doug Goodwin—RB—Mid-Eastern Shore

Dick Koeper—T—Oregon State

Junior Coffey—RB—Washington

Bud Marshall—DT—Stephen F. Austin

Jim Weatherwax—DT—Los Angeles State

Gene Jeter—LB—Texas Southern

Roy Schmidt—G—Long Beach State

Chuck Hurston—DE—Auburn

Phil Vandersea—LB—Massachusetts

1966: Losing only two of our 14 games, we once again were the world champs. We finished with five straight victories and clinched the Western Conference title by beating the Colts in the rain and mud in Baltimore by a score of 14–10. We went on to beat the Cowboys 34–27 in Dallas. In the first Super Bowl meeting between the NFL and AFL, the Packers exploded in the second half to beat the Chiefs 35–10.

1966 Draft Class

Jim Grabowski—RB—Illinois

Gale Gillingham—G—Minnesota

Tom Cichowski—T—Maryland

Fred Heron—DT—San Jose State

Tony Jeter—TE—Nebraska

John Roderick—WR—SMU

Ron Rector—RB—Northwestern
Ralph Wenzel—G—San Diego State
Jim Mankins—RB—Florida State
Dave Hathcock—DB—Memphis

Future Hall of Fame members already on the team at the time of Taylor's arrival:

*Willie Davis—1960 (from Grambling—acquired from Cleveland Browns)
*Forrest Gregg—1956 (from Southern Methodist—drafted by Packers in 1956)
*Paul Hornung—1957 (from Notre Dame—drafted by Packers in 1957)
*Henry Jordan—1959 (from Virginia—acquired from Cleveland Browns)
*Jim Ringo—1953 (from Syracuse—drafted by Packers in 1953)
*Willie Wood—1960 (Southern California—signed as a free agent in 1960)

History of the Lombardi Era: The Taylor Years (1958–1966)

1959: The Lombardi era began with a bang as the Packers defeated the Chicago Bears in the first game of the season at Lambeau Field on September 27. The Packers went on to win two more to get off to a 3–0 start. However, the young team struggled in the middle of the season, losing five straight. But the Packers rebounded and won their final four games to finish with a 7–5 record, their first winning season in 12 years.

1960: The Packers' resurgence under Vince Lombardi continued as the Packers battled for their first division championship in 16 years. Through seven games the Pack was 5–2 and sitting atop the NFL West. Two straight losses made their position precarious, but the Packers hunkered down and won their last three games to claim the Western title with an 8–4 record. In their first NFL Championship Game since 1944, the Packers faced the Eagles in Philadelphia. The Packers drove deep into Eagles territory twice but settled for field goals. The Eagles responded by scoring 10 points to take a 10–6 halftime lead. After both teams failed to score in the third, the

Packers took a 13–10 lead in the fourth quarter on a Bart Starr–to–Max McGee TD pass. However, on the ensuing kickoff the Eagles returned the ball into Packers territory, which set up the championship-winning TD with 5:21 left. The Packers made one last charge, but Chuck Bednarik stopped Jim Taylor eight yards from the end zone as time ran out.

1961: Led by an MVP season from RB Paul Hornung, who scored 10 touchdowns while scoring 86 points with his foot, the Packers cruised to their second straight Western Division championship by posting an 11–3 record. In the NFL Championship Game the town of Green Bay finally got a taste of playoff football as the Packers faced the New York Giants. A record crowd at City Stadium II watched the Packers erupt for 24 points in the second quarter. The Pack went on to claim their record seventh championship with a 37–0 white-washing of the Giants.

1962: Led by Jim Taylor, who becomes the second-straight Packer to win the NFL MVP, the Packers got off to an incredible 10–0 start. After losing to the Lions in Detroit in Week 11, the Packers got up and went on to finish with a franchise-best 13–1 record, winning the NFL West for the third year in a row. The Packers went on to face the Giants in an NFL Championship Game rematch in New York. At Yankee Stadium, the Packers used Jim Taylor to bludgeon the Giants and give the Pack an opportunity to score. Taylor and the Packers won the battle 16–7 for their second-straight NFL championship.

1963: The NFL suspended star RB Paul Hornung for one season for betting on football. Without Hornung the Packers still went on to post a strong 11–2–1 season. However, both losses came at the hands of the Chicago Bears, who beat the Packers by one game in the race for the division title.

1964: In perhaps Vince Lombardi's most frustrating year as coach, the Packers played mediocre football through the first 10 games and sat at 5–5. With all hopes of the playoffs lost, the Packers did not lose another game, but their 8–5–1 record felt like a disappointment.

1965: The Packers paid tribute to their founder, Curley Lambeau, who died during the off-season, by renaming City Stadium II Lambeau Field in his honor. The Packers rebounded from their disappointing season to challenge the Baltimore Colts for the Western Division championship. The Packers appeared to sew up the Championship by routing the Colts 42–27 in Baltimore in the next-to-last game of the season. However, the Packers were tied by the San Francisco 49ers in the final game of the season, forcing the Packers to play the Colts in Baltimore again in a divisional playoff. The playoff game against the Colts in Baltimore was an instant classic as both teams battled into overtime tied at 10. However, one OT period was not enough as the game went into a second overtime. Don Chandler's 25-yard FG a little over a minute into the sixth quarter sent the Packers on to the NFL Championship Game. In the championship game at Lambeau Field the Packers faced the Cleveland Browns on a field made sloppy by a four-inch snowfall. The two teams battled back and forth, and the Packers held a 13–12 lead at halftime. In the second half the Packers' defense clamped down, and they went on to win their ninth NFL championship 23–12.

1966: In perhaps his finest season, QB Bart Starr won the NFL MVP, leading the Packers to a 12–2 record that easily captured the Packers' fifth Western Division title in seven years. In the NFL Championship Game the Packers traveled to Dallas to take on the Cowboys. The Packers jumped out to a 14–0 lead quickly only to have the Cowboys surge back to tie the game at 14. In the second quarter the Packers pulled out in front on a 51-yard Starr pass to Carroll Dale. However, with 2 FGs the Cowboys pulled to within one point. Bart Starr then collected two more TD passes, and the Packers appeared to have the game sewn up, but a missed PAT gave the Cowboys hope, and after a 68-yard TD pass from Don Meredith the Cowboys had new life. They got to the doorstep of tying the game as time wound down, but CB Tom Brown intercepted a Meredith pass in the end zone with 28 seconds left to seal the Packers' 34–27 victory.

Super Bowl I: For the first time ever the NFL champion faced the AFL champion in a game to become the undisputed world champion of football. The game took place with little fanfare at the half-empty L.A. Coliseum as the Packers faced the AFL champion Kansas City Chiefs. The Packers struck first as Bart Starr hit Max McGee with a 37-yard TD pass. The Pack took a 14–10 lead into halftime. In the second half the Packers scored 21 unanswered points to claim the championship with a 35–10 victory.

Afterword by Jim Taylor

There Was Something Special About Lombardi

I was Green Bay's No. 2 pick in the 1958 draft, and even though the Packers had won only three games the previous year, I was delighted about it. Unlike some of the players, I liked Green Bay. Coming from Baton Rouge, I liked the small-town atmosphere. We were there to do a job, and football was the only thing on the plate in Green Bay—at least for me.

I spent most of the first 10 games playing on the special teams unit, but then Paul Hornung got injured, and I got to replace him for two straight games on the West Coast. I gained more than 100 yards in both games, and it made me feel pretty good. I thought, *Maybe I can play this game, after all.*

But then the Packers fired Scooter McLean and hired Vince Lombardi. I didn't have any particular expectations when I reported to camp. The Packers had other running backs, and I was just determined to earn a spot on the team. It didn't take long to know there was something special about Lombardi. He was a disciplinarian and, unlike McLean, he kept things simple. I was ready to be led, and I was willing to work very, very hard.

I'm just so happy that I came along in Lombardi's era. He had a lot to do with maxing me out as a player. He used intimidation to push me to the next level, just as he did with a lot of the players. It wasn't easy, but he was exactly what I needed to become as good a player as I could be.

We always looked forward to playing the Cleveland Browns and their great running back, Jim Brown. Ray Nitschke and the rest of our defense took great pride in trying to stop Brown, and that's probably the main reason he never seemed to hurt us as much as he did other teams.

Whenever we played the Browns, the media liked to make a big deal of the battle between Brown and me. I never looked at it that way. I was just trying to be the best player I could be for the Packers and do whatever the game plan called for. Oh, I guess we were competing inadvertently, but the reason I wanted to play better than Brown was to help us win, not to achieve some individual honors for myself.

Lombardi loved to beat the Giants because New York was his hometown and he had been an assistant coach at both West Point and with the Giants before coming to Green Bay. One of our sweetest wins came in the 1962 NFL Title Game when we beat the Giants 16–7 on an unbelievably cold and windy day in Yankee Stadium.

The field was frozen and the wind was swirling, and all day Sam Huff, the Giants' middle linebacker, was wearing me out. I mean, he was consistently pounding me every chance he got. I carried the ball 31 times but gained only about 85 yards. After one carry early in the game, I was hauling myself up from the ground when Huff said, "Taylor, you stink!"

I didn't say a word, but a few plays later, I scored from the 7-yard line to give us a 10–0 lead. From the end zone, I yelled to Huff, "Hey, Sam, how do I smell from here?"

Lombardi liked the way I ran. Whenever I'd get in the secondary and a linebacker or a cornerback approached me, my style was to drop my shoulder so they couldn't go for my legs. Some of the guys said I liked to attack tacklers. Maybe I did. If I knew I was going to have a collision, I had to be ready to take him out before he could take me out.

In the spring of 1966, the NFL and the AFL got into a bidding war over the crop of college seniors who were coming out. The Packers drafted Donny Anderson from Texas Tech and Jim Grabowski from Illinois, and they gave them each a huge signing bonus just to keep them from going to the AFL. I think each of them got around $150,000, maybe more.

I was making $38,500, and I was the leading rusher on the team that had just won its fourth NFL title in six years. I'd been there all that time and had tried to do the best job I could do. Lombardi tried to give me a three- or four-year contract, but I decided to play out my option.

We rolled to a 12–2 record in 1966 and beat Kansas City 35–10 in the first Super Bowl. I became a free agent, but Hank Stram, the Chiefs' coach, and a couple of the others pretty much blackballed me because I was bucking the system. But I didn't care. I took my position and held it and moved on from there.

I finally signed with the Saints but played only a year before retiring. It was a season where players were coming from all the teams, so it was difficult to get some teamwork, some timing, and some tempo. It was tough to play for a bad team after all those great years in Green Bay.

I don't know how the Green Bay Packers rank among the great NFL dynasties, but I'd say we could compete with any team of any era. Lombardi believed in *KISS*—Keep it Simple, Stupid. He worked endlessly to make us eliminate mistakes. One of the big things he promoted was total team unity. The offensive side and the defensive side all got along very well.

Lombardi wrote a famous essay entitled *The Habit of Winning*. The following is an excerpt from his thoughts:

> I firmly believe that any man's finest hour, his greatest fulfillment to all he holds dear, is the moment when he has worked his heart out in a good cause and lies exhausted on the field of battle…victorious.

Winning is what Lombardi stood for, and it was the most important principle he taught us. Not only did he teach us to win, but he taught us *how to win*. Anything less than winning was not acceptable.

Sources

Carlson, Chuck. *Game of My Life: Green Bay Packers: Memorable Stories of Packers Football.* Champaign, Illinois: Sports Publishing, LLC, 2004.

Carroll, Bob. *When the Grass Was Real.* New York: Simon & Schuster, 1983.

Carroll, Bob, Michael Gershman, David Neft, and John Thorn. *Total Football II: The Official Encyclopedia of the National Football League.* New York: Harper Collins, 1997.

Claerbaut, David. *Bart Starr: When Leadership Mattered.* New York: Taylor Trade Publishing, 2004.

Devaney, John. *Bart Starr.* New York: Scholastic Book Services, 1967.

Eisenberg, John. *That First Season: How Vince Lombardi Took the Worst Team in the NFL and Set It on the Path to Glory.* New York: Houghton Mifflin Harcourt, 2009.

Footballhistorian.com. "Packers vs. Bears—December 1960." http://www.footballhistorian.com/football_heroes.cfm?page=34 (accessed June 10, 2009).

Gruver, Ed. *Nitschke.* New York: Taylor Trade Publishing, 2002.

Gruver, Ed. "The Lombardi Sweep: The Signature Play of the Green Bay Dynasty That Symbolized an Era." *The Coffin Corner* Vol. 19, No. 5 (1997).

Gulbrandsen, Don. *Green Bay Packers: The Complete Illustrated History.* Minneapolis: Voyageur Press, 2008.

Gutowski, Tim. "Milwaukee Talks." Special to OnMilwaukee.com from October 12, 2004 (accessed June 24, 2009).

Hardesty, Dan. *LSU—The Louisiana Tigers.* Huntsville, Alabama: The Strode Publishers, 1975.

Hendricks, Martin. "Booming Play, Thunderous Legacy: Taylor's Bullish Style Helped Define Era." JS Online February 4, 2009 (accessed December 1, 2009).

Hollow, Cooper. "Happy Packers Had Many Heroes—Taylor Is MVP of Game." *Chicago Tribune,* January 2, 1966.

Hornung, Paul (as told to William F. Reed). *Golden Boy*. New York: Simon & Schuster, 2004.

Hornung, Paul and Billy Reed. *Lombardi and Me: Players, Coaches, and Colleagues Talk About the Man and the Myth*. Chicago: Triumph Books, 2006.

Johnson, Chuck. *"Taylor Isn't Human (Said Huff)."* Milwaukee Journal (circa 1960s).

Johnson, Chuck, Bud Lea, Jim Murray, Lee Remmel, and Bob Woessner. *The Lombardi Era and the Green Bay Packers (1959–1967)* (A publication of the Green Bay Packer Yearbook, 1968, by Art Daley and Jack Yuenger). Menomonee Falls, WI: Inland Press, 1968.

Kaplan, Richard. *Great Upsets of the NFL*. New York: Random House, 1972.

King, Sam. "Ex-LSU, NFL Player Taylor Doing Best to Overcome Stroke." *Baton Rouge Advocate*, July 4, 2004.

Lawrence, Andrew. "Jim Taylor, Fullback." *Sports Illustrated*, August 22, 1966.

Lea, Bud. *Magnificent Seven: The Championship Games That Built the Lombardi Dynasty*. Chicago: Triumph Books, 2002.

Lombardi Jr., Vince. *What It Takes to Be Number 1: Vince Lombardi on Leadership*. New York: McGraw-Hill Professional Publishing, 2001.

Maraniss, David. *When Pride Still Mattered: A Life of Vince Lombardi*. New York: Simon & Schuster, 1999.

Miller, Mike. "Jack Vainisi: The Drafting Genius Behind the Packers Dynasty." *The (Madison, WI) Capital Times*, April 23, 2009.

Nitschke, Ray amd Robert W. Wells. *Mean on Sunday: The Autobiography of Ray Nitschke*. Madison, Wisconsin: Prairie Oak Press, 1998.

O'Brien, Michael. *Vince: A Personal Biography of Vince Lombardi*. New York: HarperCollins, 1987.

O'Day, Joe. "Football's Furious Feud: An Irresistible Force Meets an Immovable Object." *Sports Quarterly* presents PROS Football '63.

O'Donnell, Chuck. "Jim Taylor: In Brutal Conditions at Yankee Stadium in the NFL Title Game in 1962, the Running Back Paved the Way for a Packers Victory Over the Giants—The Game I'll Never Forget." *Football Digest*, September 2002.

Pro Football Hall of Fame. "History of the Green Bay Packers." www.profootballhof.com (accessed December 15, 2009).

Pro Football Reference. "The Green Bay Packers 1957–1967." www.profootballreference.com (accessed November 15, 2009).

Sargent, Jim. "Ron Kramer, All-American: Michigan Legend, Packer Great, Lion Hero." *The Coffin Corner* Vol. 26, No. 1 (2004).

Schoor, Gene. *Bart Starr: A Biography*. New York: Doubleday & Company, 1977.

Sports.Jrank.org. "Vince Lombardi Biography: The Early Years, First Coaching Position, College Football, Chronology, Awards and Accomplishments, Moving Up With the Giants." http://sports.jrank.org/pages/2901/Lombardi- Vince.html#ixzz0KcUU3INH&D (accessed July 6, 2009).

Vandermause, Mike. "Thurston has Worthy Story to Tell." *Green Bay Press-Gazette*, October 2, 2009.

Weibush, John. "Packers Legend Max McGee Passes Away." Green Bay, Booze, and Broads, http://greenbayboozeandbroads.blogspot.com/2007/10/packer-legend- max-mcgee-passes-away.html (accessed September 29, 2009).

Whittingham, Richard. *The Fireside Book of Pro Football: An Anthology of the Best, Most Entertaining Writing About Professional Football*. New York: Simon & Schuster, 1989